Praise for The Choice Factory

"This book is a Haynes Manual for understanding consumer behaviour. You should buy a copy - and then buy another copy to give to one of the 97% of people in marketing who are too young to remember what a bloody Haynes Manual is."

— Rory Sutherland, columnist for *The Spectator,* and Executive Creative Director, Ogilvy One

"Most books in this area are academic and dry as dust. If you want to know how research and sociology can impact on real life in the real world, Richard's book will show you - using simple words and examples that real people can understand."

— Dave Trott, columnist, *Campaign*, and author of *Predatory Thinking, Creative Mischief* and *1+1=3*

"In a cacophony of overstatement, Richard Shotton possesses a melodious and balanced voice. In this short but powerful tome you can learn about how marketing actually does influence consumers. Or, for the more prosaic among us, how to get people to re-use towels, buy wine when German Oompah music is playing and select a broadband supplier by mentioning Charing Cross Station. The book also mentions me (all too briefly) which I also find enticing."

— Mark Ritson, columnist, *Marketing Week*, and Professor at Melbourne business school

"Actionable, memorable and powerful... Shotton has taken the jewels of behavioral economics and made them practical."

— Seth Godin, author of *All Marketers are Liars*

"Comprehensive, compelling and immensely practical, the Choice Factory brings the building blocks of behaviour change together in one place."

— Richard Huntington, Chairman & Chief Strategy Officer, Saatchi & Saatchi

"A top class guide for those who want to put BE to work, rather than just illuminate their journey to work. Richard pushes the practical application of these central psychological concepts. An essential handbook."

— Mark Earls, author of *Herd*

"The Choice Factory is a delightful anatomy of the biased brain that will help you understand and influence consumer decisions – including your own."

— Ian Leslie, author of *Born Liars and Curious*

Richard delivers a wealth of cases proving the efficacy of working with, rather than against, the grain of human nature. This is catnip for the industry.

— Phil Barden, author of
Decoded: The Science Behind Why We Buy

Richard Shotton's application of behavioural economics is bang on the button. This book is timely, insightful, fascinating and entertaining.

— Dominic Mills, former editor, *Campaign*

"If you're a marketer, understanding what really makes people tick – as opposed to what they might tell you – is vital. *The Choice Factory* book takes us on an elegant, witty and digestible tour of the 25 main principles of behavioural science. Richard Shotton has read widely so that you don't have to, but he gives full credit to his many sources should you wish to pursue any of the topics further. This is a delightful and indispensable read for anyone in marketing, particularly those early in their careers."

— Tess Alps, Chair of Thinkbox

The *Choice* Factory

HARRIMAN HOUSE LTD
18 College Street
Petersfield
Hampshire
GU31 4AD
GREAT BRITAIN
Tel: +44 (0)1730 233870
Email: enquiries@harriman-house.com
Website: www.harriman-house.com

First published in Great Britain in 2018
Copyright © Richard Shotton

The right of Richard Shotton to be identified as the author has been asserted in accordance with the Copyright, Design and Patents Act 1988.

Paperback ISBN: 978-0-85719-609-5
eBook ISBN: 978-0-85719-610-1

British Library Cataloguing in Publication Data
A CIP catalogue record for this book can be obtained from the British Library.

The *Choice* Factory

How *25 behavioural biases* influence the products we decide to buy

By Richard Shotton

Hh Harriman House

Every owner of a physical copy of this edition of

The Choice Factory

can download the eBook for free direct from us at Harriman House, in a format that can be read on any eReader, tablet or smartphone.

Simply head to:

ebooks.harriman-house.com/choicefactory

to get your free eBook now.

Contents

Preface

What this book covers

The Choice Factory is an overview of how findings from behavioural science can be applied to advertising. Behavioural science, the study of decision-making, is an important topic for advertisers as it provides a robust explanation about why people buy particular products.

It recognises that people are overwhelmed by the sheer volume of decisions they need to make each day. People don't have the time or energy to laboriously and logically weigh up each decision. Instead, they rely on short-cuts to make decisions more quickly. While these short-cuts enable quicker decision-making, they are prone to biases. These biases are the subject of this book.

If advertisers are aware of these biases, and adapt their products and communications accordingly, then they can use them to their advantage. They can work with the grain of human nature rather than unproductively challenging it.

A number of successful brands – including Apple and Volkswagen – are applying behavioural science, but they're in the minority. There's an opportunity for you to gain an advantage by harnessing behavioural science before your competitors.

Behavioural science has identified a remarkably broad, and ever-growing, range of biases. This breadth means that whatever your communication challenge, there's normally a relevant bias that can help solve it.

This book is not an exhaustive list of all the biases that have been discovered by behavioural science. I have been selective and focused on the 25 most relevant biases to advertising. All the biases covered can be easily applied to your campaigns to make them more powerful.

Who this book is for

The Choice Factory is primarily aimed at professionals working in advertising and marketing, whether at an agency or a brand. It'll give you practical advice on how to apply behavioural science in your work. However, if you run your own business or you have a general interest in behavioural science, there will be plenty to interest you.

How this book is structured

The book is split into 25 chapters, with each chapter covering a specific bias. You can read the chapters in order, or if you prefer, you can dip in and out – jumping between the chapters that you think are most relevant.

Throughout the book we'll be following a single person through their day, looking at the decisions they make. Each chapter starts with a short paragraph detailing one decision. These range from the incidental, such as what beer to order at the pub, to the substantial, such as who to hire at an interview. The person we'll follow through the day should be of interest to you – it's you.

I'll explain why you made your decision by referencing one specific bias. I'll explain the academic and real-world evidence for the bias. This evidence is more robust than many of the theories that shape advertising decisions. It's based on the peer-reviewed experiments of some of the world's leading scientists. Academics such as the Nobel Laureates, Daniel Kahneman and Herbert Simon, as well as respected psychologists such as Elliot Aronson and Leon Festinger.

When discussing the evidence, I'll pull out the nuances. These are particularly interesting as they are not very well known; if you apply them it'll give you an advantage over your competitors.

After interrogating the existing evidence I'll cover my own experiments in the field. This is important as they bridge the gap between academia and practice. My experiments prove that behavioural science is relevant today and that it applies to commercial situations as much as non-commercial ones.

Most importantly, I'll focus on what you should do with this knowledge. This is the bulk of each chapter. I'll show you how you can apply behavioural science to your advertising, whether that's the message, who you target or when you reach them. These findings are easier than ever to apply as the increase in digital advertising means that it's cheaper and quicker than ever to test new approaches and easier to monitor their success.

Hopefully, the book will pique your interest in behavioural science. If it does you'll find recommendations for further reading, as well as references for all the studies quoted, at the back of the book. As it's an ever-expanding field I also tweet links to any interesting new research I discover from the twitter handle @rshotton.

Introduction

How applying the findings of social psychology improves marketing

THE INSIDE OF a stuffy black cab crawling along Oxford Street isn't a place suited to epiphanies. Nevertheless, on a swelteringly hot day in 2005, that was where I read the story that would change the way I thought about advertising.

The tale was that of Kitty Genovese. Her stabbing, and the psychology experiments it inspired, convinced me that behavioural science could shake up advertising.

Kitty's story was a bleak one. At 3.20 am on 13 March 1964 she began walking the 100 feet from her car to the entrance of her apartment in Kew Gardens, New York. Unfortunately, as she made her way along the tree-lined street, she was spotted by the serial killer, Winston Moseley. Moseley, a 29-year-old father of two, shadowed her, until, a few yards short of her door, he plunged a knife into her back.

This single murder wasn't enough to shock New Yorkers: after all, there were 636 murder victims in the city that year. It was the events of the next few minutes that so shook the city and led the *New York Times* to dedicate a front page to the incident. According to the paper:

> For more than half an hour, 38 respectable, law-abiding citizens in Queens watched a killer stalk and stab a woman in three separate attacks in Kew Gardens.

> Twice the sound of their voices and the sudden glow of their bedroom lights interrupted him and frightened him off. Each time he returned, sought her out and stabbed her again. Not

one person telephoned the police during the assault; one witness called after the woman was dead.

The supposed apathy of the witnesses scandalised the city. Why did no one intervene?

While many of the details of the article were later challenged, the story sparked the interest of two psychologists, Bibb Latané and John Darley. They wondered if the commentators had interpreted the problem the wrong way around. It wasn't that no one intervened *despite* the volume of witnesses; no one intervened *because* there were so many bystanders.

The academics spent the next few years testing their hypothesis. I'll look at their results in more detail in Bias 24, but suffice to say they proved that the broader an appeal for help, the less likely any individual is to intervene. They termed this diffusion of responsibility the *bystander effect*, although it's sometimes referred to as the *Genovese syndrome*.

A practical application

It struck me that these findings related to a problem I was grappling with. At the time, I was working as a media planner and one of my clients was the NHS and their *Give Blood* campaign. They regularly ran appeals warning of low blood stocks across the country. But these campaigns weren't generating as many donations as hoped. If the psychologists were right, then the NHS's broad appeals were suffering from the bystander effect.

Perhaps it would be more effective to run specific appeals?

Fortunately, the creative agency team working on the campaign were open to suggestions. The team, led by Charlie Snow, agreed to test regionally-tailored digital copy. This meant that rather than the ads saying, "blood stocks are low across the UK please help", they were adapted to say, "blood stocks are low in Basildon (or Brentwood or Birmingham), please help".

Two weeks later the campaign results arrived. There was a 10% improvement in the cost per donation. The simple application of a 40-year-old bias had improved a modern ad campaign.

This was a revelation for me.

I'd finished studying at Oxford University half a dozen years earlier and since then I'd ignored academia on the assumption that research was irrelevant to the hard nosed, commercial world of advertising. But I was mistaken. What could be more relevant to advertising – which aims to change the decisions of consumers – than a study of the roots of decision-making?

As Rory Sutherland, Vice Chairman, Ogilvy & Mather Group, says:

> This subject provides a robust, intellectual link between understanding human nature and knowing how to make money.

In the same way that you wouldn't trust a doctor with no knowledge of physiology or an engineer ignorant of physics, my experience over the last dozen or so years suggests that it's foolhardy to work with an advertiser who knows nothing of behavioural science.

One of the most significant discoveries I've made over that time is the variety of biases that are covered in the field. There's no single, grand theory underpinning behavioural science. Instead, there's a broad collection of biases.

This has two benefits. First, it means that whatever brief you're tackling there's likely to be a relevant bias to harness. Second, it avoids the danger of making our tasks fit the solutions at hand, rather than the other way around.

Robust as well as relevant

Behavioural science provides answers to many advertising conundrums. But more important than this relevance is the robustness of the findings. The field is based on the experiments of some of the most respected scientists of the day: Nobel Laureates like Daniel Kahneman, Herbert Simon and Robert Shiller.

This evidence-based foundation contrasts with many marketing theories which are based on anecdote or tradition. Byron Sharp, Professor of Marketing Science at the University of South Australia, has been highly critical of marketers' reliance on untested assumptions. He has compared the situation with medieval bloodletters who shunned experimentation:

> The study of marketing is so young that we would be arrogant to believe that we know it all, or even that we have got the basics right yet. We can draw an analogy with medical practice. For centuries this noble profession has attracted some of the best and brightest people in society, who were typically far better educated than other professionals. Yet for 2,500 years these experts enthusiastically and universally taught and practised bloodletting (a generally useless and often fatal 'cure'). Only very recently, about 80 years ago, medical professionals started doing the very opposite, and today blood transfusions save numerous lives every day. Marketing managers operate a bit like medieval doctors – working on anecdotal experience, impressions and myth-based explanations.

Since behavioural science is based on experiments, you don't have to take the findings on faith alone. The methodologies used to test each bias are openly available and you can repeat them to ensure they work for your brand.

I've spent the last 12 years testing existing biases to determine how they can best be used by brands. It's the findings of these tests that I'd like to take you through in this book.

A competitive advantage

Despite the relevance and robustness of behavioural science, the results are erratically applied in marketing.

Consider the placebo effect. This is the finding that if patients expect a drug to work, it's more likely that it will, even if the medicine has no active ingredients. One of the most interesting facets of placebos is that small, seemingly incidental, details such as the pill's price, size, taste, even the colour can dramatically boost the size of the effect.

Anton de Craen, a clinical epidemiologist at the University of Amsterdam, conducted a systematic review of 12 studies and found that red painkillers were consistently more potent than blue ones. This is due to the cultural connotations of each colour; while red suggests strength and power, blue evokes calming images of the sky and sea. For a painkiller strength is more important than calmness.

Analgesics are a high-value market. According to Euromonitor, £614m was spent on analgesics in the UK in 2016. However, many painkillers fail to fully capitalise on the placebo effect. Of the seven packs of painkillers I purchased on a string of visits to Boots, a measly one was red. What a waste. Why do so many brands ignore the opportunity, when a small design twist could improve performance?

Part of the reason behavioural science findings are sometimes ignored is that advertisers often ask consumers directly about their motivations. It seems a logical enough approach. However, it's based on the premise that what consumers say and what they do are aligned. Unfortunately, as we'll see through the book, that's often not the case. As the New York University psychologist Jonathan Haidt says, the conscious brain thinks it is the Oval Office but it is actually the press office.

Few consumers admit that they'd be less likely to help a stranger if others were asked at the same time, or that their headache would disappear faster with a different coloured pill. Yet, when we watch how consumers actually behave, it's apparent that we are affected by such nuances.

While ignoring behavioural science is bad news for the industry it is good news for you. It means that if you apply the findings then you'll have a competitive advantage. Let's turn to some of those lessons now.

BIAS 1

The Fundamental Attribution Error

Why brands need target contexts
as much as target audiences

You slam your front door closed and trudge towards your car, which owing to a lack of off-street parking is a hundred yards away. In between you and the car is a beggar, slumped in a doorway.

A stream of busy commuters walks past him without stopping. You watch as a man, dressed in a pinstripe suit, picks up his pace, averts his gaze and strides past the vagrant. Good god – people are so selfish today, you think.

You root around in your pocket for some change to donate. There's only a fiver so you pick up your pace and avert your gaze.

YOUR ASSUMPTION ABOUT the selfishness of the businessman is an example of the fundamental attribution error. That's the tendency to overestimate the importance of personality, and underestimate that of context, when explaining behaviour. You judged the businessman's actions with reference to his personality rather than fleeting factors like his mood, busy-ness or mindset.

This mistake is widespread and has important implications for how we think about targeting our communications.

The classic experiment

In 1973 two Princeton University psychologists, John Darley and Daniel Batson, published a landmark paper on the topic entitled: *From Jerusalem to Jericho*. The paper proved how seemingly incidental contextual factors had a significant, but under-appreciated, influence on behaviour.

They asked 40 trainee Catholic priests to complete questionnaires regarding their motivation for entering the church. The surveys unpicked whether the students were motivated by helping others or to ensure their own salvation.

Once the surveys were completed the psychologists told the priests to record a five-minute talk on a given topic. Since the current room had insufficient space the students were sent, armed with a map, to see another colleague in a building a few minutes away.

Just before the participants left, they were notified how much time they had until the recording. A third of the students were told, "Oh, you're late. They were expecting you a few minutes ago. We'd better get moving. The assistant should be waiting for you so you'd better hurry." This was the high hurry condition.

Another third, those in the intermediate hurry condition, were warned, "The assistant is ready for you, so please go right over." And the final third, in the low hurry condition, were told, "It'll be a few minutes before they're ready for you, but you might as well head on over. If you have to wait over there, it shouldn't be long."

The students were randomly, and separately, allocated to the different conditions.

As the participants marched, or strolled, towards their destination they passed a confederate of the psychologists. The stooge pretended to be in distress. He was slumped, head down with his eyes closed in a doorway and as a student approached he groaned and coughed.

This was the crux of the experiment. Which students would stop and help?

The power of the situation

Overall, 40% of the participants stopped. The primary determinant was how time-pressured they felt. In the high hurry condition, a mere 10% stopped, compared to 45% in the intermediate condition and a full 63% in the low hurry condition.

In contrast, the personality metric had minimal impact. It didn't matter to any sizeable degree why someone had elected to join the priesthood. The situation, not the person, determined the behaviour.

Do the findings still apply nearly 50 years later?

A lot has changed since then. In 1973 a pint of beer cost 14p, Smash Martians were advertising instant mash and Tim Berners-Lee, inventor of the web, was still at school.

But despite these differences our underlying motivations remain. As Bill Bernbach, the legendary creative, said:

> It took millions of years for man's instincts to develop. It will take millions more for them to even vary. It is fashionable to talk about changing man. A communicator must be concerned with unchanging man, with his obsessive drive to survive, to be admired, to succeed, to love, to take care of his own.

Yet agencies continue to peddle the myth that consumers have radically changed.

Why?

It's often due to their vested interests, rather than the underlying truth. According to Bob Hoffman, the outspoken author of *Marketers are from Mars, Consumers are from New Jersey*:

> The more they can convince us that everything is changing, and we need them to interpret the changes -- the longer they stay employed. And so they have created an avalanche of exaggerated claims and dire warnings that gain them attention and a nice little profit from the increased viewership/listenership/readership.

But don't just take Bob's word for it. Through this book I'll demonstrate the unchanging nature of people. To do that I'll replicate, or build on, many classic experiments and prove that they still apply today.

We consistently underestimate context

The Darley experiment proved that in that particular situation context trumped personality. But that jars with most people's prediction of what would happen.

Laura Maclean and I engaged 433 people in a thought experiment. Imagine, we said, a man slumped in a doorway, possibly in need of help, who do you think will stop? A caring man in a rush or a not so caring one with plenty of time?

It wasn't even close. 81% thought those in a rush were more likely to stop. Only 19% predicted those with plenty of time. Pretty much the opposite of the results of Darley's experiment.

Why do we underestimate context as a driver of behaviour? Perhaps, because it boosts our self-image: it appeals to our ego to believe that we are paragons of rationality. Who wants to admit to being at the whim of external forces?

If Darley's was the only experiment that showed people underestimate the importance of context then it would be sensible to treat the findings with caution. However, this finding has been repeated in a broad range of circumstances, perhaps most famously by Lee Ross, Professor of Social Psychology at Stanford University.

Ross recruited 36 students to take part in a quiz; half were randomly allocated to the role of questioner and the remainder were the contestants. The questioners had 15 minutes to think of 10 tricky questions on a topic of their choice and then the contestants had to answer them as well as they could. As might be expected most contestants struggled to answer many of the mind-boggling questions. Finally, the participants had to rate each other's general knowledge.

Contestants rated their questioners' general knowledge as significantly higher than the questioners rated the contestants. Both parties mistakenly attributed the other person's performance to their personality rather than the context of the situation.

How to apply this effect

1. Research little and often

Laura and I used Google Surveys to conduct our thought experiment. A single question among a nationally representative group costs about 7p per person and the data is normally available in one or two days.

The growth in these opportunities is a boon for brands. Research no longer needs to be limited to large projects conducted once a year. Instead, it can be used to address the daily questions that marketers have.

2. Those in a rush are distracted

The rushing students in the experiment were less helpful. The Princeton psychologists thought one reason was a "narrowing of the cognitive map", a phrase they borrowed from University of California – Berkeley psychologist, Edward Tolman.

According to Darley:

> Our seminarians in a hurry noticed the victim in that in the post-experiment interview almost all mentioned him, as on reflection, possibly in need of help. But it seems that they often had not worked this out when they were near the victim.

They were so focused on the pressing engagement that it crowded out their ability to fully process other information.

One simple lesson is to avoid communicating when people are rushing.

There are circumstances where inattention is beneficial, such as in persuading those who dislike your brand, and we'll investigate those in Bias 11. However, by and large, advertisers should prioritise attentive audiences. The simplest lesson from the experiment is to avoid communicating when people are rushing.

This principle is supported by an experiment by CBS Outdoor and TNS, a major research company, in 2008, aptly named *Total Recall*. They recruited 290 participants off the street to take part in interviews. Some were led directly to an interview room, passing through a corridor lined with poster ads on the way. Others were held in a waiting room full of posters for three minutes, before being taken via the same corridor to the interview room. Once in the room they were asked to recall the ads.

The difference in recall between those with three minutes ad exposure and those with three seconds was extreme. Compared to the low dwell-time group, those who had a longer exposure to the ads were six times more likely to recall the ad, four times more likely to remember details and a whopping fourteen times more likely to correctly remember the brand in question.

The data from *Total Recall* was based on the length of time ads were in view. However, just because something is in view it doesn't mean it was viewed. The impact of viewing time on recall has been quantified recently by eye-tracking company, Lumen Research. They have analysed 100,233 impressions of print ads and shown that if an ad is viewed for less than a second only 25% of people recall it, whereas if that ad is seen for between one and two seconds recall jumps to 45%. The company founder, Mike Follett, argues that advertisers must aim for their ads to be seen for at least one second.

That sounds like an easy benchmark to beat. However, further data from Lumen Research shows that most online advertising falls short. They have a panel of 300 people who have agreed to have eye-tracking software installed on their computers. This allows Lumen to analyse how long people look at ads for when they're browsing naturally. Their analysis of 53,962 impressions shows that 4% of display ads are looked at for more than one second.

Advertisers cannot assume their online ads will be seen for at least a second. They need to seek out the domains and formats that deliver long view times. For example, there is a six-fold difference in the average length of time that ads on major sites are viewed for. According to Lumen, the viewing of ads on online sites of the national press are particularly high.

The fact there is such a variation in how long impressions are viewed suggests advertisers should re-evaluate how they buy media. At the moment the standard metric is cost per thousand – how much it costs for a thousand impressions – but Lumen data suggests advertisers should consider trading on time spent.

3. Target contexts as well as target audiences

The most important finding from this experiment is that contextual factors are often more influential than personality in determining behaviour. This undermines one of advertising's most deeply held beliefs: that brands must identify and then focus their communications on a core target audience.

The experiment suggests that brands should focus as much on target contexts as they do target audiences. Throughout the book I'll be examining how contexts encourage certain behaviours.

4. Don't assume you know the right context

The Darley experiment had a final twist. Think back to the set-up when the psychologists asked the students to give a talk. What I didn't mention was that half were asked to discuss the parable of the Good Samaritan, and half the jobs best suited to graduates.

The parable concerns a traveller robbed, beaten and left for dead on the road from Jerusalem to Jericho. Three religious men pass by: a priest, a Levite and a Samaritan. The first two regrettably ignore him, only the Samaritan stops.

As religious students, the participants would have known this parable well. "It is hard to think", said Darley, "of a context in which norms concerning helping those in distress are more salient than for a person thinking about the Good Samaritan." It would be reasonable to expect that those due to speak about the Good Samaritan would be particularly likely to stop. But that wasn't the case. The sermon topic made not a jot of difference.

Context is crucial. But what particular context is not obvious. We need to subject our hypotheses to simple tests to see the effect on our brand, in our market. As the Nobel Laureate, Richard Feynman, said:

> It doesn't matter how beautiful your theory is, it doesn't matter how smart you are. If it doesn't agree with experiments, it's wrong.

One social psychology theory that is both beautiful and supported by plenty of experimental evidence is social proof. It's there we turn next.

BIAS 2

Social Proof

*Why popular brands become
more popular still*

As you drive to the station you spot a huddle of pedestrians staring up at a tree. You crane your neck round to see the cause of the excitement. A stranded cat, maybe? Or perhaps the tree is about to be felled? Before you find out, the lights change and on you go.

YOU'RE BEING INFLUENCED by social proof, becoming interested in an event because others are. It's an established bias first noted in the 1935 study by Muzafer Sherif, one of the founders of modern social psychology.

While Sherif's work is interesting, it is recent work conducted by Robert Cialdini that is most relevant to marketers. Cialdini, a professor of psychology and marketing at Arizona State University, persuaded an American hotel chain to adapt the messages they left in guests' rooms trying to encourage towel re-use. He created three different messages. The first, his control message, which stated the environmental benefits, was successful among 35% of visitors.

The social proof message, in contrast, simply stated that most people re-used their towels. This version, shorn of any rational message, boosted compliance to 44%. An uplift of 9% points, or 26%, is impressive, especially when it required no extra spend. Most marketing campaigns deliver more modest results.

Does the bias apply in business?

A recent experiment I conducted suggests social proof is relevant elsewhere. I showed 300 respondents images of a fake beer brand and told them it was launching in the UK. Half were told about the origin of the ingredients and half were told the same story but with the additional information that it was South Africa's most popular beer. In the second scenario, consumers were twice as likely to want to try it.

Richard Clay and I tested the effectiveness of social proof in a bar. South London's Canopy brewery agreed to place a small sign on their bar saying the porter was this week's best-selling ale. This boosted sales by a factor of 2.5 compared to an average week. When we stripped out fluctuations in weekly sales this represented a doubling in the proportion of porter sales. A real-life experiment like this is the ideal place to test biases as it removes the doubt that the biases are a product of the laboratory environment.

How to apply this effect

1. State popularity

The simplest approach is to clearly state the popularity of your product. Many famous campaigns have done so, with Whiskas being the most prominent. Their long running campaign claimed: "Eight out of ten owners said their cats prefer it". Unfortunately, a complaint to the Advertising Standards Authority meant this was toned down to the less pithy, but more accurate: "Eight out of ten cat owners who expressed a preference said their cats preferred it".

This basic approach can also be used at point of sale to reassure customers. McDonald's famously displayed restaurant signs saying how many had been served – 1 million in 1955, when Ray Kroc bought the company, to 99 billion in 1994.

2. Tailor the claim

Shouting about popularity works, but you can be even more effective, as shown by the next phase of Cialdini's experiment. He ran a third message asking people to re-use their towels because most people in their room had done so. This boosted re-use rates to 49% – an increase versus the control of 40%. Cialdini argued that the message was more effective because it was more relevant. The relevance in his experiment was tenuous to say the least; imagine how much more effective messages can be if they harness genuine relevance.

> The best tactic is to state your brand's popularity in a relevant way to your audience.

Instances of advertisers applying this tailored approach are rarer. However, Costa, the UK's largest coffee chain, is one such example. Their ads refer to their popularity, not among drinkers, but coffee lovers. This ensures the ad resonates with those who class themselves as connoisseurs. The *Guardian* reported that this boosted sales by 5.5% on a like-for-like basis – impressive growth for a mature brand.

The best tactic is to state your brand's popularity in a relevant way to your audience. One way is to run regional messages. For example, saying your Manchester's favourite to Mancunians. Another approach is tailoring your claim to the publication you're appearing in. When your ad appears in the *Guardian* you mention the popularity among their readers, but in the *Daily Mail* it's *Mail* readers that you reference. Get those two audiences muddled and you might regret it.

If it's so effective, why isn't it more common?

The evidence for social proof is robust – so why is it a rare tactic? On the day I wrote this I flicked through the *Times* and found only a single ad harnessing social proof. Why?

The main reason is that when brands contemplate what message to run they commission a survey. Invariably respondents claim that

> The way to improve your research is to stop just listening to what customers say and start looking at what they do.

other people have no influence whatsoever, that they make their decisions independently. That is normally the end of most proposed social proof campaigns.

A final twist in Cialdini's towel experiment suggests brands are too hasty. Cialdini contacted a group of students and asked which of the towel re-use messages would be most persuasive. Overwhelmingly, they plumped for the environmental message. The opposite of how people actually behaved. Naively believing customers will mislead you. As David Ogilvy said, "Consumers don't think how they feel, say what they think or do what they say."

And yet advertisers still conduct research as if claims can be taken at face value. Most market research money is spent on surveys. The way to improve your research is to stop just listening to what customers say and start looking at what they do.

In the words of Mark Earls, author of *Herd*, "We need to learn from anthropology and focus on the space between people not the space between their ears."

3. Don't assume your scale is known

The second reason is that many brands assume their popularity is known. The marketers responsible for the ad are well aware of their market share and too often they falsely assume shoppers are too. This is a mistake. Claire Linford and I surveyed 1,003 consumers about who the leading brand was in each of four categories: cars, instant coffee, draught lager and coffee shops. For three of the four categories, only a minority answered correctly. This was most extreme for draught lager, where only 24% knew that Carling was Britain's best-selling pub pint. If you're popular don't assume people know – shout about it!

4. Think creatively

Another barrier to social proof is that most brands aren't market leaders. There's only one number one. But with a little creativity, this doesn't need to stop you. Take chocolate bars. You can reference the number of sales, such as the age-old claim on Tunnock's wrappers that five million are sold weekly. Or you could talk about sales growth – perhaps you're the fastest growing. Or perhaps you're successful in a sub-category – maybe you're market leader in dark chocolate bars. There are hundreds of possible permutations.

There are innovative ways of formulating a marketing claim. But there are also creative ways of expressing that claim. In the right hands a potentially dry message can be made more powerful. For example, Jeremy Bullmore, ex-Chairman of JWT, describes Ford in the 1970s wanting to promote their convertible's popularity:

> They could perfectly well have said: "America's bestselling convertible". Instead they ran a headline that read: "The only convertible that outsells Ford." And the picture was of a baby-carriage. That is a kind of humour; and it's almost a joke. It certainly depends entirely on a contribution from the audience for the communication to be complete. But the contribution is a small and pleasurable one, well within the capacity of anyone in the market for a car. And what could have been a piece of self-congratulatory manufacturer's so-whattery became engaging evidence of confident leadership. The point had been seen.

The brands who take the time to convey their social proof messages with charm and wit will be even more successful.

Tapping into social proof doesn't even require facts. Your task is to create the illusion of popularity. In 2001 when Apple launched the iPod, the competitors all had bland, black earphones. When the mp3 player was tucked in a listener's pocket, passers-by had no idea which make was being listened to. Their success was invisible.

In contrast, iPod owners were easily identifiable with their striking white headphones. Their distinctiveness made Apple look like the market leader long before it was, which made the brand that much more desirable. As Guy Kawasaki, Apple's former Chief Evangelist, said, "the bottom line is that familiarity breeds commitment, not contempt." When Business Insider looked back at the iPod's phenomenal success they claimed that "perhaps the company's greatest innovation was … those all-white earbuds."

The iPod was not an isolated example. Magners tapped into social proof when they launched in the UK. They were the first brand to serve their cider over ice, which meant that even after the drink had been poured, and the bottle disposed of, it was obvious what punters were drinking. In the summer of 2005 this distinctive approach created the illusion that everyone was drinking Magners, which made them more popular still. The marketing plan cleverly amplified this impression by launching one region at a time. They saturated each region in turn until it felt like Magners was the must-have drink.

5. Get your priorities right

The final, often unstated, barrier is that social proof appears simplistic. Our professional pride is piqued by such an easy solution. Applying it doesn't make us feel intelligent, a cut above salesmen. But to bow to these considerations is to elevate our interests over those paying for the ads. It's a muddling of priorities. What matters is whether social proof sells. And on that count the evidence is conclusive.

Social proof is an influential but under-used approach. However, its power can sometimes backfire – and that's the topic of the next chapter.

BIAS 3

Negative Social Proof

When a bias backfires

You arrive at the station, car park flustered, but with a few minutes to spare. When the train pulls in there are a handful of empty seats left. If you can edge your way in quickly you might get one. Luckily, when the train clatters to a halt, the doors are directly in front of you. A seat is yours.

After a few minutes of idle thought, you get your phone out and flick through the main news headlines. Your browsing is interrupted by a plea from the *Guardian*, "more people are reading The *Guardian* than ever, but fewer are paying for it". You ignore the message and search in vain for the tiny 'x' that will get rid of the ad.

THE *GUARDIAN'S* INEFFECTUAL request has fallen victim to what Robert Cialdini, Professor of Psychology at Arizona State University, terms "negative social proof".

As discussed in the previous chapter, social proof describes how consumers are significantly influenced by the behaviour of others. Negative social proof is the inadvertent misuse of the bias. It's when social proof is used in such a way that it has the opposite effect to that intended.

Negative social proof in action

The evidence for the bias originates from an experiment conducted in 2003 in Arizona's Petrified Forest National Park by Cialdini and two of his colleagues, Steve Martin and Noah Goldstein. They chose this location as, at the time, a ton of petrified wood was being stolen each month. This rate was so calamitous that the site was one of America's ten most endangered national parks.

The park rangers reacted by erecting signs that declared:

> Your heritage is being vandalised every day by theft losses of petrified wood of 14 tons a year, mostly a small piece at a time.

But were these signs effective? Since they emphasised the number of thieves, the psychologists worried they encouraged more stealing.

The team tested this hypothesis by placing petrified wood at three spots close to paths in the park. On two of the three routes, they erected signs to discourage stealing, while the third was left sign-less as a control.

The first sign, which warned of the impact of stealing, stated:

> Please don't remove the petrified wood from the park, changing the natural state of the Petrified Forest.

The second sign read:

> Many past visitors have removed the petrified wood from the park, changing the natural state of the Petrified Forest.

This was the negative social proof message, as it emphasised how widespread inappropriate behaviour was.

When people saw the sign condemning theft, 1.7% of the pieces were stolen. In contrast, that figure jumped to 7.9% when there was a negative social proof message. That's more than four times the rate.

Even more worryingly, the negative social proof message led to twice as many thefts as when there was no advertising at all. In the control situation, when there was no message, the rate of theft was only

2.9%. That means a sign designed to reduced crime, boosted it. In Cialdini's words, "This wasn't a crime prevention strategy; it was a crime promotion strategy."

Too many campaigns are victims of negative social proof

Many social marketing campaigns still shock people with daunting figures about the scale of the problem they're trying to solve. They're so commonplace that Cialdini terms it advertising's "big mistake".

Consider Wikipedia who are currently raising funds with the following on-site message:

> We'll get right to it: this week we ask you to help Wikipedia. To protect our independence, we'll never run ads. We're sustained by donations averaging about $15. **Only a tiny proportion of our readers give**. If everyone reading this right now gave $3, our fundraisers would be done within an hour. [My highlighting]

Or the NHS's Give Blood campaign that publicises that only 4% of people donate blood. David Halpern, Chief Executive of the government's Behavioural Insight Team, goes as far as to say he has lost count of the number of examples he has seen:

➻ posters telling immigration officers that some of their colleagues had been caught and punished for selling work visas ("Never thought of that – I wonder how much they made?"),

➻ signs in doctors' surgeries about the number of people who missed their appointments in the last month ("… so I'm not the only one"), and

➻ national campaigns bemoaning the low number of women on top company boards ("well,

> Communications fail when they stress that an unwanted behaviour is commonplace.

we've got a woman on our board of 12, so that's pretty good, then").

These communications fail because they stress that the unwanted behaviour is commonplace. Unfortunately, as we're social animals who mimic others, that encourages the very behaviour they're trying to stop.

How to apply this effect

1. Flip the statistics

The same situation can be described in different ways. Make sure your description emphasises the popularity of the desired behaviour.

Don't emphasise the 14 tons of stolen petrified wood; communicate that 97% of visitors don't steal.

Don't talk about only 4% donating blood; honestly claim there are two million donors but more are needed.

In each situation try to choose a number that harnesses social proof positively not negatively.

2. Close the gap between perception and reality

Our actions are shaped by how we think others behave. However, those estimates are often inaccurate.

For example, in 2014 IPSOS MORI asked 1,000 adults in the UK to estimate the scale of various social issues. The respondents were consistently wide of the mark. The sample estimated 16% of 15 to 19-year-old girls gave birth each year. The real figure, according to the United Nations, is less than a fifth of that: 3%.

Similarly, the average estimate was that a mere 49% of eligible adults voted at the last general election. The real figure was a much healthier 66%.

The media, charities and governments often talk in such panicked terms about social problems that the public overestimate their prevalence. Rather than seeking to exaggerate the issue, check whether perceptions diverge from reality. If so, close the gap.

3. Talk about the injunctive, not the descriptive norm

There are two types of norm: those referring to how you *should* behave, called injunctive norms, and those describing how *most* people behave, known as descriptive norms. If you are faced by a situation where most people are behaving in an undesirable manner, one option is to use injunctive norms rather than descriptive ones.

For example, if a minority are donating to the *Guardian* or *Wikipedia*, an alternative is to publicise the view that freeloading is frowned upon. I surveyed a nationally representative group and, of those who offered an opinion, 62% believed that it was unfair to use a news site without paying if they had been requested to do so.

But that's enough discussion of how social biases can backfire. Let's turn to a more positive application of behavioural science, specifically distinctiveness – one of the most valuable tactics a brand can apply…

BIAS 4

Distinctiveness

When the world zigs, then zag

You slowly shuffle towards the station ticket gate, a part of the throng of passengers dressed in greys, blues and blacks. As you finally reach the turnstile your eyes are drawn towards one of the staff on duty. The man, probably in his 50s, looks like an old punk: head shaved to the scalp apart from a two-foot-tall bright blue Mohican. You wonder idly what would happen if you turned up to work with a Mohican?

OF COURSE, YOU noticed the Mohican, rather than one of the hundreds of short back and sides. You're hard-wired to notice what's distinctive. The academic evidence for this dates back to 1933 and the experiments of a young, postdoctoral student, Hedwig von Restorff.

Restorff was a paediatrics researcher at the University of Berlin when she published her study on memorability. She gave participants a long list of text: it consisted of random strings of three letters interrupted by one set of three digits. So, for example: jrm, tws, als, huk, bnm, 153, fdy. After a short pause the participants were asked to remember the items. The results showed that items that stood out, in this case the three digits, were most recalled. This is known as the Von Restorff, or isolation, effect.

Unfortunately, soon afterwards Von Restorff's career was cut tragically short. The Nazis conducted a purge of the university and she, along with many other psychologists, was thrown out. Hedwig, who wasn't even thirty, never published again.

Still relevant today

But that experiment was more than 80 years ago – do the findings still stand? My colleague, Laura Weston, and I investigated. We gave 500 nationally representative participants a list of numbers: 15 written in black, one in blue. A short time later we asked which number they recalled. Respondents were 30 times more likely to recall the distinctive number.

We repeated the experiment with brands – respondents saw a list of logos: eleven car brands and a fast-food brand. Again, after a pause we asked which brands they could recall. Consumers were four times more likely to mention the fast-food brand than the average car brand. Being distinctive makes brands memorable. This might sound like an obvious point but it is one that is studiously ignored by the advertising industry.

How to apply this effect

1. Subvert category norms

Much advertising slavishly abides by category norms. Copernicus Consulting analysed 340 TV ads that ran in peak-time TV in 2001 and identified a differentiating brand message in only 7% of them.

You can see the herd mentality in action in lager. The leading brands invariably sponsor football. In 2012 four of the largest properties were sponsored by lager brands: Carling were sponsoring the League

Cup, Budweiser the FA Cup, Heineken the Champion's League and Carlsberg were the official beer of the England team. Such was the clutter that *Campaign* magazine said they are "playing 11-a-side on a 5-a-side pitch".

The same lack of variation is in evidence in other categories. Car ads are prone to loving shots of the model rounding bends in the rugged countryside. Fashion ads feature beautiful people pouting at the camera. Watch ads take it the furthest. Almost every ad shows the same time on the watch: a few minutes either side of 10:10. That specific time was chosen because the hands clearly frame the logo. The HTC phone ads run 10:08 on the time on their screens – even though it's displayed digitally!

Mimicry comes at a cost. According to Vic Polkinghorne, founder of creative agency, *Sell! Sell!*:

> What might seem like a safe choice in the confines of a boardroom will most likely be a waste of money when it's out in the real world. Advertising that feels safe or familiar is actually quite risky – there's no "safety in numbers" when it comes to advertising. If someone else is doing something similar to what you're doing, or looks or sounds like you, you're both in trouble.

Your task, therefore, is to identify the formulaic rules of behaviour in the category you work in and subvert them. The rewards can be immense, as the case of comparison sites reveals. In 2008 the main brands followed the same tactics. Gocompare, Moneysupermarket, Confused and Comparethemarket all focused on their functional benefits – how many insurers they compared and how much they saved the average consumer. Undoubtedly, these are important benefits, but as everyone was claiming them they conferred no commercial advantage.

In January 2009 Comparethemarket broke ranks. Instead of relentlessly communicating rational benefits they followed a more emotional route. They created the anthropomorphic meerkat, Aleksandr Orlov, who owned Comparethemeerkat. The ads told the tale of how his site kept crashing because of all the people mistyping Comparethemarket. The results were impressive. It rose from fourth ranked site to first in terms of consideration and spontaneous awareness. Quote volumes went up by 83% and the company achieved its 12-month objectives in 9 weeks. Distinctiveness paid.

One of my main memories from working with Comparethemarket was how small their marketing team was. They had a tight group of two or three decision-makers. I'm sure this was a factor in their success. The more people involved in a process the less likely it is, in my experience, to be distinctive. Committees are not conducive to original work. As the comedian Allan Sherman said, "They sit there in committees day after day, and they each put in a colour and it comes out gray".

2. Consider your target audience's age

Richard Cimbalo and Lois Brink, from Daemen College and the University of Colorado respectively, conducted a study in 1982 into the influence of age on the Von Restorff effect. Seventy-two college students and pensioners memorised a list on which one of the items was distinctive. As expected the distinctive item was the most memorable but the effect was more pronounced among the younger group.

Advertisers who target younger age groups need to be particularly aware of this and apply it regularly.

3. Why is distinctiveness so rare?

Why, despite the evidence, do few brands break conventions? Dave Trott, the illustrious creative director says:

> The problem is nobody ever explains to clients why the obvious is bad. They think it must be right because everyone in their market is doing it. Which is exactly why creatives think it's wrong. Creatives want to be different, to stand out from the

environment. But that just looks like flashy pyrotechnics to a client.

However, distinctiveness is more than 'flashy pyrotechnics'. Perhaps agencies in their rush to promote the latest fad have forgotten to emphasise the fundamentals? Agencies must publicise the work of Von Restorff to prove the power of being distinctive.

However, there's another, more intractable, issue – if you're distinctive and the campaign fails then you could get them fired. "Especially for junior clients", says Trott, "the safety is in doing what everyone else is doing."

If the campaign flops they can point to the behaviour of their competitors as a sign that they undertook due diligence before approving the ad campaign. Ironically, brands have sought to capitalise on this defensive decision-making in their own communications. The line, "No-one ever got fired for buying IBM", regularly acclaimed as one of the best ad slogans ever, tapped into these personal concerns.

The final explanation is a myopic approach to data. In my experience, many brands want examples of successful case studies from their category before they commit to a course of action. This leads to mimicry. If, say, all lager brands sponsor football then there will be examples where it has worked. However, if no brand sponsors, say, table-tennis, there will be a dearth of examples. This leads to a vicious circle in which more brands plough money into football regardless of the odds of success.

Brands must seek inspiration from beyond their category. If they do so they will see one of the common factors of the few brands who have created a genuine step-change in their category is that they were highly distinctive. As the founder of BBH, John Hegarty put it in his ad for black Levi's "when the world zigs, zag".

Unfortunately, Hegarty has never commented on the best way to disrupt customer habits. We'll have to muddle through the next chapter on our own.

BIAS 5

Habit

---

*How to disrupt behaviour when
most of it is unthinkingly habitual*

> You make your way across the concourse to the tube entrance, weaving your way through the crowds. There's a longer queue in the ticket hall than normal as one of the escalators is broken. Everyone must walk down it as if it were a set of stairs.
>
> After patiently queuing for five minutes you're finally at the top of the escalator, ready to go down. As you walk on to the metal steps you feel a momentary sense of unease and imbalance. But it quickly passes and on you go...

CAN YOU REMEMBER the last time you walked up a broken escalator? It was disconcerting, wasn't it? There's a momentary loss of balance as you step on. Even though you know the steps are frozen you can't help but step on too fast, thrusting your chest forward to compensate for the momentum you normally encounter.

This "broken escalator phenomenon", described by Raymond Reynolds, from the University of Birmingham, occurs because through repeated experience we've developed a habit that we can't fully override.

These habits account for a significant proportion of our actions, but they're normally invisible; revealed only when our environment changes.

Marketers need to adapt their communications to harness the power of consumers' habits.

Nearly half of behaviour is habitual

The scale of habitual behaviour was quantified in a diary-based experiment conducted by two psychologists, Jeffrey Quinn and Wendy Wood, from Duke University. They gave 279 undergraduates watches programmed to buzz at set times. Whenever the alert was triggered, the students recorded in detail their actions at that moment. Across a range of areas from exercising to travelling, from eating to socialising, a full 45% of behaviours were habitual – the same decisions being made at the same time and place without full conscious thought.

This poses a problem for brands. How do you persuade people to buy your brand if most of the time they are on autopilot, thoughtlessly buying the same product as last time?

Habits are hard to break

Since habits are context specific, if a consumer's environment changes the habits become loosened. For example, when consumers undergo a life event, their environment is changed enough to destabilise habitual behaviour. In case that term is unfamiliar, by *life event* I mean important changes, such as getting a new job, starting university, having a baby or getting married.

To quantify the importance of these moments, my colleague, Laura Weston, and I surveyed 2,370 nationally representative customers. We asked two questions. First, which life events they had undergone recently. Second, whether they had changed brands in ten specified categories. The categories straddled a diverse range of sectors: make-up, taxis, trains, coffee shops, lager, broadband, cars, mobiles, even opticians. We then cross-referenced the two sets of answers – more reliable than asking directly, as people often don't know their motivations.

The results were conclusive. We investigated ten product categories and six life events for each, so there were sixty variables in total. For every single one, consumers were more likely to switch brands when they had undergone a life event.

It was a sizeable effect too. On average 8% of consumers switched brands in the selected categories when they hadn't undergone a major life event recently. This rose to 21% among those that had. For three categories, those who had undergone life events were more than three times more likely to have switched brands.

How to apply this effect

1. Shake consumers out of automatic behaviour

The most direct approach is to draw consumers' attention to a habit and jolt them out of their behaviour. The key to success is to target communications to the moment or place this automatic behaviour happens.

One successful example was Sainsbury's in 2004 who realised much supermarket shopping was done in a daze. "Sleep shopping" as they termed it. Shoppers were buying the same items week in, week out – restricting themselves to the same 150 items, despite there being 30,000 on offer.

AMV BBDO, Sainsbury's creative agency, went to great lengths to dramatise the extent of sleep shopping. They hired a man dressed in a gorilla suit and sent him to a Sainsbury's to do his week's shopping. They questioned shoppers as they were leaving the store and a surprisingly low percentage had noticed him. When shoppers are on autopilot it's hard to grab their attention.

The agency tried to wake customers from their doze with their campaign, Try Something New Today, which used Jamie Oliver to inspire shoppers to be more adventurous. The ads were complemented by recipe cards in store, point-of-sale signage and a training programme for all 150,000 staff.

The campaign was a success – but disrupting habits is not easy. It worked for Sainsbury's because, as a retailer, they controlled the environment in which the habitual actions occurred. This meant they could harness more point-of-sale material than any packaged good could ever afford. Additionally, they committed their entire, and sizeable, ad budget to the task. Habits are hard to break.

2. Target customers after they have undergone a life event

As habits are hard to break, brands should identify the rare moments when their grip becomes loosened, such as when consumers undergo life events. These moments are easier than ever before to identify because of the wealth of targeting data available. Facebook, for example, captures when users move to a new house or end a relationship.

Life events such as retirement shake up purchasing behaviour among older consumers just as powerfully as younger ones. This offers an opportunity for you to target the notoriously immovable older audience. Since they switch brands less often, the brief window just after a life event may be disproportionately important.

Finally, identify the life event most relevant to your category. The relative importance of life events varies by category. For example, for make-up, the crucial ones are when a consumer changes their social group – when they start a job, start university or get divorced. In these circumstances, buyers might need a confidence boost or take the opportunity to forge a new look.

3. Advertise at moments of reflection

Adam Alter and Hal Hershfield, psychologists from New York University and UCLA respectively, have identified a surprising moment when people are more likely to reappraise their lives – when their age ends in nine. They term this group: "nine-enders". The psychologists analysed data from the 42,063 respondents to the World Values survey and found nine-enders were more likely to question the meaningfulness of their lives.

This moment of greater reflection occurs because we don't think of time progressing in an even manner. Certain landmarks, such as approaching a new decade, assume disproportionate importance.

Jenny Riddell and I wanted to see if the findings held in the UK. We surveyed 500 nationally representative adults and found that nine-enders were 12% more likely to claim to think issues through thoroughly.

Interestingly, for marketers, this introspection often leads to action. Many nine-enders address their predicament by taking quite drastic steps. Having affairs for one thing. The psychologists analysed the ages of eight million male users of a website, ashleymaddison.com, which specialises in arranging affairs for those in a relationship. (Its cheery slogan: "Life is short. Have an affair.")

They found that men were 18% more likely to have an affair when their age ended in nine. If men are more likely to reflect on their lives it's therefore more likely that they realise something is amiss and take remedial action.

Unfortunately, the self-destructive behaviour doesn't end there. Data, from the US Center for Disease Control and Prevention, showed a small, but statistically significant, increase in the number of nine-enders committing suicide.

Not all the behaviour is negative though.

Nine-enders are just more likely to make big, decisive steps, good or bad, to change their lives. Data from the sports website athlinks (www.athlinks.com) showed that they were 48% more likely to enter marathons for the first time than other age groups.

If you need to get consumers to reappraise their behaviours, nine-enders may be a particularly appropriate group to talk to.

4. Communicate before habits harden

An alternative approach is to focus communications before habits become entrenched.

An example from social policy illustrates the benefits. In the US, David Olds, Professor of Paediatrics at the University of Colorado, developed an intervention, called Nurse Family Partnership, which provided nursing support to vulnerable mothers until their child turned two. Every fortnight a nurse would visit the low-income families and provide health, developmental and nutritional advice. Rigorous testing has shown that this significantly reduced violence and improved educational results. However, these impressive results only occurred with mums having their first child. There was no effect on those having their second or third child as the habits were set by then.

This isn't a one-off. The same scenario can be seen with government attempts to encourage small businesses to pay their tax on time. According to David Halpern, CEO of the UK government's Behavioural Insight Team:

> The problem… is that once someone gets into the habit of paying their tax late, or not paying it at all, it's quite hard to get them to change. They've got used to receiving numerous letters, and "shoves" such as fines, rather than being nudged. It's no surprise that one extra phone call or nudge will have less effect.

The benefits of targeting people before habits become fixed extends to commercial brands. They should give disproportionate emphasis to category entrants. So, for supermarkets, families with older children might be the biggest spenders, but the retailers should recognise a better long-term approach might be those shopping for groceries for themselves for the first time: such as students and first jobbers.

Another tactic that can be used by supermarkets, and retailers in general, to boost sales is to make their prices appear less painful. This doesn't mean they must reduce prices, just that they need to take care when communicating them. That's the topic for the next chapter.

BIAS 6

The Pain of Payment

*How your price can be made
to feel less painful*

By ten o'clock you're feeling sluggish, your attention
wandering off before you reach the end of an email.
Time for a caffeine hit. But as the office coffee machine
is broken (when isn't it?) you have to pop to the local
café. You order a skinny flat white and then, just before
paying with your card, you impulsively treat yourself to
some millionaire's shortbread. Or, as they grandiosely
call it, billionaire's shortbread. It's three quid, but what
the heck.

WHY DID YOU treat yourself? Could paying by card have
encouraged you? Evidence from Duncan Simester and Drazen
Prelec suggests so.

In 2001, the MIT professors held an auction for a pair of basketball
tickets among 64 MBA students. Each student had to submit their
maximum bid for the tickets. As with most experiments, there was
a twist: half the participants were told they must pay by credit card;
half by cash. When paying by card, the average bid was $61 – more
than double the cash offer of $29.

You might reasonably object at this point that the card premium was due to students having access to more funds. However, other elements of the experiment suggest that's not the case. First, they had been told there was a cash machine nearby. Second, when the experiment was repeated with lower value basketball paraphernalia students bid $5.29 when paying by card, compared to $3.32 for cash. The fact they still bid more when paying by card on such easily affordable items suggests that access to funds wasn't a key factor. Some other reason was at play.

People paying with cash typically overestimated their spend by 9%.

The psychologists' hypothesis was that paying by card dulls the pain of payment. When consumers pay with cash the cost of the good is far more salient, paying by card masks that sensation. In the words of NYU Stern School of Business researchers, Priya Raghubir and Joydeep Srivastava, this leads to credit cards being treated like "monopoly money".

In a rare flash of academic humour the authors titled their paper *'Always Leave Home Without It'*, a dig at the AMEX strapline that warned *'Don't Leave Home Without It'*.

What about new payment technologies?

Recently we have seen a flurry of new payment methods – the most widespread of which are contactless cards. Gabrielle Hobday and I investigated how contactless cards affected price sensitivity by posing three questions to people leaving coffee shops in Central London:

➻ How much did you spend?

➻ What means of payment did you use?

➻ Please can we see your receipt?

The last question was crucial, as it let us compare recollection with reality.

The findings were striking. People paying with cash typically overestimated their spend by 9%, whereas those using contactless cards underestimated by 5%. A stretch of 14 percentage points. Credit card estimates were, in contrast, spot on.

The variation is important: on a typical supermarket shop of £25, the 14% difference between recollections of spend on a contactless card and cash amounts to £3.50. Contactless cards could be the difference between remembering a shopping trip as expensive or cheap. It is this memory that determines whether shoppers return. A positive recollection can either be achieved by steep discounting, which erodes profits, or by an innovative approach to payment.

How to apply this effect

1. Invest in cashless payment technology

Contactless terminals still haven't been universally adopted. Too many retailers regard them as an unnecessary cost, rather than an opportunity to encourage sales. If you haven't introduced them at your retail outlets, do so quickly.

But don't worry, changing price perceptions doesn't require costly, complex technology. Any means by which you can distance the consumer from the tangibility of money will reduce price sensitivity. It's one of the reasons why casinos use chips rather than cash. The little plastic discs don't feel like real money so gamblers become that little bit more frivolous with them.

One simple application is for brands to put more effort behind selling pre-paid gift cards. Like casino chips and credit cards these are one step removed from cash so shoppers tend to splash out on them a bit more.

2. Extend the principle to your visuals

Paying contactlessly is just one example of a broader opportunity – that of making the same price appear smaller. Price perception is affected by how the number is displayed. For example, an experiment by Sybil Yang, Sheryl Kimes and Mauro Sessarego from the Cornell Center for Hospitality Research proved that removing the dollar sign from menus boosted sales by 8%. Just as cards reduce the tangibility of the price, so does removing the dollar sign.

Upmarket restaurants have long followed this principle but chains, such as Byron and Café Rouge, are now catching on. However, they are still in the minority and the odds are that your business could benefit from this tweak too.

Perhaps an 8% improvement seems inconsequential to you? If so, remember that there are no activation costs so it's pure profit. Additionally, adopting this approach doesn't preclude using others; if you apply multiple biases the savings quickly mount.

3. Consider charm pricing

A complementary approach to the removal of pound signs is charm pricing, that is setting prices to end in a nine, whether that is £3.99 or £39. Shoppers tend to think goods sold for these amounts are better value than those with rounded prices.

I surveyed 650 consumers about their value perception of six different products. Half saw prices ending in 99p, while the remainder saw prices a penny or two higher. Charm prices were 9% more likely to be seen as good value than the rounded prices. A disproportionately large improvement for a 1% price drop.

If anything, my experiment underestimated the power of 99p. In real-life shopping, the bias is exacerbated because customers are in a rush. In 2013 Gumroad, a platform that lets creators sell directly to the public, analysed all the items on their site under $6, where the price ended in either 99c or a round dollar figure. They compared those items' conversion rates, that is, the number of people who bought the item divided by the number who looked at it. The conversion rate for items with a charm price was 3.5%, compared to 2.3% for those priced at a 1% premium. That's a difference of 51%.

But why are charm prices so effective?

One explanation is the *left digit effect*. Since we read from left to right, we give undue prominence to the first digits in a price. So, for example, when you're out shopping you might simply remember a price, like £3.99 as £3.

However, a study by Eric Anderson and Duncan Simester, from the University of Chicago and MIT respectively, suggests it's not the only factor.

In 2003 they partnered with a mail order retailer to test the impact of different prices on the sales of dresses. The retailer created three different versions of their catalogue and tweaked the price of four dresses. In the control version of the catalogue the dresses were priced at $39,

Removing the dollar sign from menus boosted sales by 8%.

$49, $59 and $79. In this scenario, they sold 66 dresses in total. In the first test catalogue, the dresses were sold for $5 more, so the $39 dress was priced at $44. Sales dropped to 45 dresses. However, in the final test catalogue dresses were sold for $5 dollars less than the control, so, for example, $34 rather than $39. In this scenario, they sold 46 dresses.

The left digit effect explains why the $39 price point sold more than the $44 one but not why $39 outsold $34. Another factor must be at play. The most likely explanation is that repeated exposure to sales and prices ending in a nine has led to a strong association between that price and a bargain.

Whatever the explanation there is a strong rationale for considering charm pricing. This might at first sound an obvious point. Haven't retailers been using these tactics for hundreds of years? That's true, but some retailers are turning away from charm pricing.

I analysed 650 supermarket prices tracked by Brand View and found that prices are three times more likely to end in zero than a nine. Some supermarkets actively avoid prices ending in nine. I looked at 528 additional Sainsbury's prices and found that only 1.5% ended in nine – far less than the 10% that chance alone would suggest.

The research into charm pricing might be long-standing but that doesn't mean businesses are always applying it.

4. Manipulate the time frame

Another approach that minimises the pain of payment is adjusting the time frame that you use when talking about your deal. I conducted an experiment to understand this further. I showed 500 consumers a genuine financing deal for Mazda and they rated the deal on a variety of metrics.

The twist was that participants saw the price displayed in one of four ways – either as a daily, weekly, monthly or annual figure. For example, £4.57 per day or £32 per week. In all cases the total worked out to the same annual amount: £1,668.

The results revealed that the shorter the time frame, the more appealing the deal. When the prices were shown as a daily figure they were five times more likely to be rated as a great deal than when they were shown annually. When compared to monthly rates the daily deal was 28% more likely to be referred to as a good or great deal.

When calculating a deal's desirability, consumers overemphasise the sum quoted and place too little weight on the time frame. Think how striking this is. It's as if consumers repeatedly estimate 6×4 to be smaller than 4×6.

The results are of direct interest to car makers but they apply to any brand offering a time-based contract, whether that's gyms, mobiles or car insurance. Deals appear better value simply by shortening the time frame around which they're communicated.

5. The power of stories

Brands know blunt approaches don't work best in ads. The need for story-telling is one of the most widely accepted pieces of industry wisdom. And yet most promotions are remarkably direct: two for one, 50% off and the like. This direct promotional approach is flawed; brands need a story for their promotions, just as they do for their TV ads.

The evidence for this comes from the US in 2005, when many car brands offered an interesting deal – the public could get the same discount as employees. Sales surged to unprecedented levels. Nothing surprising in that you might think – wasn't this just a price cut boosting sales?

But when Meghan Busse, Duncan Simester and Florian Zettelmayer, academics from MIT and the Kellogg School of Management, investigated they discovered a curious anomaly. In the previous weeks the car companies had been cutting prices so much that the employee discount was generally no better, and occasionally more expensive, than existing deals.

The academics hypothesised that it was the price cue, not the price, which mattered. Consumers reacted to the plausibility of the deal rather than the actual discount. When consumers don't trust brands they treat deals sceptically, but when they're accompanied by a back story they have more heft.

When you are contemplating promotions don't rely on an eye-watering discount. Numbers leave customers cold. We're not natural statisticians – stories move us to action far better.

However, don't expect consumers to admit how important stories are. What consumers say and what they do are often at odds. That discrepancy is the focus of the next chapter.

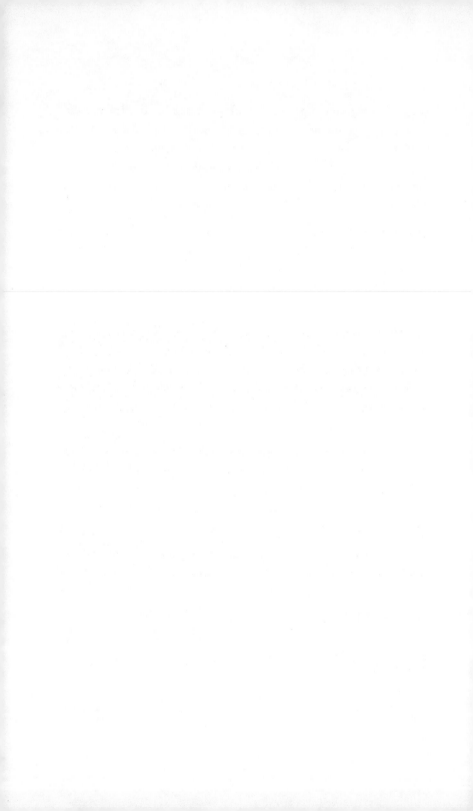

BIAS 7

The Danger of Claimed Data

*How do we know the truth
when everyone lies?*

After a busy morning, you deserve a break. You log into *Guardian* Soulmates to check your messages. Just the two. Neither seems eye-catching so you don't reply.

You're not getting as many enquiries as you expected. Perhaps you should update your profile? The first thing you change is your photo to a more flattering one, although it is a few years old.

What next? The problem is that everyone else exaggerates, so anyone looking at your profile will assume you do too. Perhaps by being scrupulously honest you're not conveying the truth.

You tweak your personal information by adding a couple of extra inches onto your height. Maybe that's overkill – you readjust your height to add just one inch. Then you change your job title. You're already doing the work of a director, probably best to call yourself one.

YOU'RE NOT ALONE, by any means, in stretching the truth to breaking point on your dating profile. Christian Rudder, founder of dating site *OK Cupid*, analysed the profiles of 1.51 million active users and uncovered evidence of systematic lying.

Men on the site are four times more likely than others of the same age and postcode to claim they earn more than $100,000. Suspicious, but not as fishy as the fact that the average height of users was supposedly two inches taller than the population average.

Most innovatively, Rudder examined the age of uploaded profile photos. When digital cameras take photos they attach text tags, called EXIF metadata, to the jpeg. These tags capture the date and time. Rudder found that while the average photo was 92 days old, the photos rated as 'hottest' were much older.

Sex, lies and survey data

If Rudder's study hinted at lying, the National Survey of Sexual Attitudes and Lifestyle (NATSAL) categorically confirms it. The survey, conducted among 15,000 respondents by UCL and the London School of Hygiene and Tropical Medicine, is the gold standard of research. In 2010 it found that British heterosexual women admit to a mean of eight sexual partners, compared to twelve for men. The difference is logically impossible. If everyone is telling the truth the mean for each gender must be the same.

All of this goes to show that advertisers trying to understand their customers have a problem: if they listen uncritically to consumers, they'll be misled.

Even honest answers can be misleading

To complicate matters, people often don't know their genuine motivations. This is demonstrated by an experiment led by Adrian North, then a psychologist at Leicester University.

Over a fortnight he alternated the background music played in a supermarket wine aisle, between traditional German oompah music and French accordion music. He surveyed customers who had bought either French or German wine. When accordion music was played, French wine accounted for 77% of wine sales; when the soundtrack was oompah music, German wine represented 73% of sales.

The scale of the variation shows that music was the prime determinant of the type of wine bought. However, only 2% of buyers spontaneously attributed their choice to the music. Even when prompted, 86% of people stated that it had no impact at all.

It's not that they were lying; more that they were unaware of their motivations. The reasons proffered were mere post-rationalisations or, in the psychological term, *confabulations*. In the memorable words of Jonathan Haidt, author of *The Righteous Mind*, the rational mind "thinks of itself as the Oval Office when actually it's the press office".

How to apply this effect

1. From lies, learning

Lies can be illuminating.

Take the NATSAL study that investigated how many sexual partners men and women admitted to. The claims are untrue but they reveal gender expectations about promiscuity. Men exaggerate their promiscuity, while women downplay it. The changing ratio between men and women tells a tale too. In 1990 men claimed to have two and a half times more sexual partners than women, by 2010 the gap had dropped to 50%. Gender expectations are levelling out.

Statistics are not transparent. They need to be teased, analysed and probed. Taking them at face value will mislead you. But if you dig further, then insights can be uncovered.

2. Adapt your surveys

Louis Heren, foreign correspondent at the *Times* famously advised, "When a politician tells you something in confidence, always ask yourself, 'Why is this lying bastard lying to me?'". His scepticism ensured he probed and pushed politicians until he uncovered the truth.

Similarly, you need to be prepared for deceit, and design surveys accordingly.

There are a couple of useful techniques. First, consider asking respondents how they think others might behave.

> # You need to be prepared for deceit, and design surveys accordingly.

I used this approach when investigating whether people feel dissatisfied by the idealised images projected on social media. Of the 300 consumers I surveyed 26% said they had pretended to be happier, or more successful, than they actually were. Furthermore, just over a third claimed to have felt unhappy when they saw others' success on social media.

While this was a sizeable proportion of the sample, I had a hunch that it was an underestimate. After all, there's a pressure to present a positive image in surveys. Psychologists call this the "social desirability bias".

With that in mind, I asked another two questions: Did they believe other people crafted an overly positive social media image? And did other people feel sad when they saw these idealised images?

In this variant of the question, people were far more likely to admit "social airbrushing" happened. In fact, 60% claimed that their friends portray themselves as happier than they actually were on social media. And nearly two-thirds agreed that other people sometimes feel sad when they see their friends' success on social media.

My belief is that these questions encouraged respondents to answer more honestly and therefore the results are more accurate.

3. Don't ask, observe

Direct questioning is unsatisfactory because of lying and confabulation. A more accurate alternative is to observe behaviour.

This could still involve surveys. The twist is to mask the objective of the question from the participant by adopting a cell methodology. This technique involves randomly allocating your sample into different cells, or groups, and then asking each group a slight variant on the question. Think back to the last chapter and the survey I ran about how different time frames affect the appeal of deals. That survey used a cell methodology. None of the participants knew that other people had been asked the survey in a slightly different way.

Even better, avoid surveys and monitor behaviour in a realistic situation. One example of this was on a New Look brief, when they were planning to launch a menswear range. The initial plans were for a modest budget to make a simple announcement.

I suspected a small campaign would be insufficient to overcome men's reluctance to buy clothes from what was perceived as a women's clothes shop. However, that was a hunch and we had no budget to fund a survey.

As an alternate methodology Dylan Griffiths and I recruited half a dozen agency volunteers and photographed them twice: first holding a New Look plastic bag emblazoned with their logo, then one while holding a Topman bag. We uploaded the images to Badoo, a dating site where people rate the looks of other users' photos. The pictures were left up on the site for a fortnight while we waited for them to be rated.

We found that when our volunteers were holding a New Look bag they were seen as 20%-25% less good-looking than when they were clutching the Topman bag. This demonstrated that the brand had a more significant job than they had initially suspected, and that they needed to make bigger efforts to persuade men that they were a unisex brand.

The final approach is to use found data. That is the data that consumers unwittingly create when they're going about their daily tasks. The data is particularly useful as it's not muddied by the social desirability bias. People aren't aware they're being monitored so they behave naturally.

Search is the most accessible found data source. Analysing search data provides insights that consumers might be loath to admit in a survey. Consider sexism. Most people would claim that they're equally interested in their children's intelligence, regardless of gender. However, Seth Stephens-Davidowitz, the *New York Times* journalist and data scientist, has analysed US search data and found that parents are two and a half times more likely to Google "is my son gifted?" than "is my daughter gifted?". Google acts as a modern confessional in which all our darkest thoughts are captured.

However, this rich seam of data is too rarely mined by advertisers. One of my favourite freely available, but untapped, search tools is answerthepublic.com. This looks at the most common search strings that include the term you give it and a question word, such as who, what, how or when. It is a very simple but quick way to understand what consumers genuinely think about your category.

For example, if you input the term 'vitamin' you find that consumers rarely search for vitamins by their letter symbol. Instead they search for vitamins by what they do, such as helping with muscle growth or shiny hair. That's a useful insight for a vitamin brand as it suggests they should label and package their vitamins according to the problem they solve, not the particular vitamin they contain.

4. Observed data is not perfect

Observed data is a significant improvement on surveys. However, it is far from perfect and still needs to be interpreted with caution.

Consider social media data. Brands regularly analyse their Facebook fan data to understand their customer profile. But this data does not always accurately reflect reality. An example from Stephens-Davidowitz illustrates this discrepancy. He looked at the gender of

Katy Perry Facebook fans and found that they were overwhelmingly female. However, Spotify listening data revealed the gender split was more balanced: Perry was in the top ten artists for both genders. If the music label used the Facebook data to target their advertising they'd be way out.

Does that mean the new data streams are junk and best ignored?

Not at all. Observed data is an improvement on claimed data, but it's still flawed. To understand customers we need a balanced approach, using multiple techniques. If each technique tells us the same story then we can give it greater credence. If they jar, then we need to generate a hypothesis to explain the contradiction.

Let's go back to the Katy Perry example. A simple explanation would be that while both genders enjoy listening to her, far more women are comfortable expressing that publicly. If a record label wants to sell Katy Perry songs or encourage streaming, then Spotify data would be ideal. However, if they want to promote her concerts, it would be better to use the Facebook numbers. Neither data set is right in any absolutist sense – they are right in certain circumstances.

Hopefully, learning about those techniques to better analyse customer claims has put you in a good mood. If it has, then beware. You'll be more susceptible to advertisers' blandishments. We'll find out why in the next chapter.

BIAS 8

Mood

*The benefit of targeting your ads
according to the consumer's mood*

You slam down the phone with a curse. The client on the conference call was being completely unrealistic. No, not unrealistic, that's the wrong word - impossible.

You begin writing an email to backtrack from what you've agreed to. But you're so annoyed you worry you'll regret sending it. Instead, you grab your coat and head outside for fresh air. Maybe that will calm you down.

You stomp down the stairs and through reception - all the while rewriting the email in your mind. Unfortunately, as you storm out you fail to spot an old friend sitting in reception that you have been keen to catch up with for ages.

THE IMPACT OF mood on our capacity for noticing has been investigated by Fred Bronner, Professor of Media and Advertising Research at the University of Amsterdam. Bronner asked 1,287 participants to flick through a newspaper and then answer questions about which ads they remembered.

When the data was split by the readers' mood the results were conclusive. Those who were relaxed noticed 56% of ads, far more than the 36% noticed by those who were stressed. Similarly, those who strongly agreed with the statement that their day "had gone super" noticed 46% of ads. In contrast, those who strongly disagreed with the statement only remembered 26% of the ads. Consumers who were in a relaxed frame of mind or a good mood were much more likely to notice the ads.

Mood doesn't just influence recall

I ran an experiment with Laura Maclean that suggests receptivity to ads grows when people are in a good mood. The experiment was simple, involving just two questions. First, we showed 2,035 people an ad and asked them how much they liked it. Then we asked them to rate how they were feeling at that moment on a scale from zero, miserable, to 10, very happy.

The results were significant. When consumers were happy (scoring seven or more on our scale), 21% of them like the ad. In contrast, only 13% of unhappy people (scoring six or less) liked the ad. That's a 62% swing in the liking of the ad.

Our results are not a one-off. Yahoo recruited 600 adults to fill in a week-long smartphone diary that tracked their moods. This revealed that when consumers are upbeat they are 24% more receptive to content in general. Nigel Clarkson, Managing Director of Yahoo UK, said:

> Digital marketers all appreciate the importance of reaching the right person, on the right device, at the right time. But the 'right time' should be about more than the webpage they're viewing at that moment. We should be striving to take a consumer's emotions into account as well.

But why should consumers be more receptive to ads? Daniel Kahneman, the Nobel Prize winning psychologist, suggests an

Bias 8 | Mood

evolutionary explanation for this phenomenon. When we are in a good mood it signifies an absence of danger and, therefore, mitigates against the need to think critically. We're therefore far more likely to absorb ad messages when we're happy.

How to apply this effect

1. Target consumers when they're likely to be happy

Since people recall ads better when they're in a good mood then brands should target this moment. There are a number of opportunities. First, consider targeting consumers during enjoyable activities. Consumers are more likely to be in a better mood at the cinema than commuting.

Second, identify particular times of day when consumers are at their happiest. For example, Touchpoints, a detailed survey conducted by the IPA, asked 5,000 consumers to keep a diary about their mood. This showed that people are most likely to be in a good mood between Friday and Sunday. This peaks on a Saturday when consumers are 40% more likely to be in a good mood than compared to the average day. Focusing your ads to these happier moments is a relatively straightforward task.

> Consumers are more likely to be in a better mood at the cinema than commuting.

2. Target consumers when you know they're happy

But these techniques are crude. They identify moments when the population is more likely to be content. They don't definitively identify an individual's mood.

However, this is starting to change. Digital signals can indicate whether consumers are happy. The creator of Snickers chocolate bars, for example, recently began targeting its ads by mood, believing that people who are happy, bored or stressed are more likely to snack. It identified these moods by mining information captured by Google's ad server, DoubleClick.

One particularly interesting area of research relates to how websites can gauge our emotions from how we move our mouse. Jeff Jenkins, Assistant Professor of Information Systems at Brigham Young University, conducted three experiments on this topic among 271 participants. His team manipulated the emotions of participants and then tracked how they scrolled their mouse as they browsed an ecommerce site. They found that the mouse movements were more jagged and sudden when participants were in a bad mood. Jenkins claims:

> Using this technology websites will no longer be dumb, they can go beyond just presenting information, but they can sense you. They can understand not just what you're providing, but what you're feeling.

3. Match your message to the mood

Mood targeting is more than just reaching consumers when they're buoyant. There is evidence that matching messages to a viewer's mood boosts effectiveness. Keith Wilcox, Professor of Marketing at Columbia Business School, conducted an experiment in 2015 among 142 participants into mood congruence.

The participants were either primed with a neutral clip, a documentary about Einstein, or a heart-rending scene from the 1979 movie, *The Champ*. The clip was followed by an ad, either a highly energetic one or a moderately energetic one. When the moods clashed participants paid less attention to the ads.

Wilcox says:

> When you feel low or sad, ads that are high energy are difficult to watch. So you spend less time watching, and the ad is less effective.

Across this and five other similar studies Wilcox found that people who were made to feel sad responded 50% better to moderately energetic ads than highly energetic ones. These experiments suggest that advertisers should seek out mood states that are congruent with their tone.

One way of putting shoppers in a good mood is to make them feel like they've bagged a bargain. But what exactly is a bargain? As you'll see in the next chapter whether or not an item is thought of as a bargain depends on what it's compared to.

BIAS 9

Price Relativity

*Make your brand appear better value
by changing the comparison set*

Feeling peckish, you go to Tesco Metro to buy lunch.
You head to the crisp aisle in search of a large bag to
share with the team. Tyrell's Salt & Vinegar are your
favourites but they're expensive - twice the price of
Walkers. But, on the other hand, Walkers just aren't as
crunchy. You deliberate for a second or two, and then
you spot the Tesco Finest. Crunchier than Walkers and
better value than Tyrell's. Choice made.

A s your visit to the crisp aisle reveals, you don't evaluate options
in isolation. Products are hot or cold, long or short, cheap or
expensive, not in absolute terms, but in comparison with other items.
This relative approach even determines how we see objects.

In the 1890s, Herman Ebbinghaus, Professor of Psychology at the
University of Berlin, created the famous illusion below.

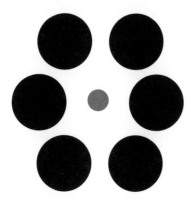

There are two identically sized circles in the centre, but it doesn't seem that way. The perceived size of the central dot depends on what it's compared to. Contrast it with large dots and it looks little; contrast it with miniature dots and it looks massive. This illusion and others like it fascinate psychologists. Nobel Laureate Daniel Kahneman, for example, spent his early career investigating them. The field is compelling because just as there are visual illusions, so there are cognitive illusions.

Price illusions on the supermarket shelves

A series of experiments I have conducted reveal that our mind's perception of value is just as relative as our eyes' perception of size. Over the last couple of years I have asked thousands of consumers to rate the value of many different brands. Invariably, their answers were shaped by the items the brands were compared to.

In one test, I told consumers that a 250g box of PG Tips cost £2.29, while the same weight of Tesco own label tea cost £1. In this scenario, 31% of the audience thought the PG Tips was good value. I then asked another group the same question but with one tweak. Rather than compare PG Tips to own label it was contrasted with Twining's, priced at £3.49. In this scenario, the number who thought PG Tips represented good value more than doubled to 65%. I found similar results for ice cream.

The relativity of our judgements is not limited to low value items bought with minimal consideration. In a separate study I told people that a Ford Mondeo cost £20,495 and a BMW 5 Series cost £30,265. In this scenario only 33% of the audience thought the BMW was good or very good value. I then asked another similar group of consumers the same question but with one change. I swapped the Ford Mondeo for a Bentley Flying Spur priced at £118,651. In this scenario, 47% of people thought the BMW represented good value. This result holds true on every car I tested. When compared to a higher priced brand, even an expensive car looks better value.

A more radical shake-up

Perceptions of value can be tweaked by altering the competitors in the comparison set. However, I wanted to discover if willingness to pay could also be shifted.

I ran an experiment among my colleagues using King Cobra, a little known variant of Cobra lager. It's a strong Indian beer, with an ABV of 7.5%, and it comes in a 750ml serving, the same size as a wine bottle.

A little subterfuge was required. I told my colleagues that we needed to run some tastings for a client. I organised two separate tastings of the beer alongside half a dozen other drinks. The participants rated the taste of the drinks on a scale from one to ten and said how much they'd be prepared to pay for each one in a supermarket.

The twist was that in each tasting Cobra was served alongside a different selection of drinks: in the first case bottled beers; in the second wines. The accompanying drinks had a significant effect on the amount people were prepared to pay for Cobra. When it was accompanied by bottled beers they offered £3.75, but when it was served with a selection of wines that rose, by 28%, to £4.80.

The presence of wine increased willingness to pay because it established a different comparison set to beer. It's acceptable to pay around a fiver for a bottle of wine, whereas few would ever countenance that much for a bottle of lager. When drinkers then estimated how much they'd be prepared to pay for King Cobra, they started from the price benchmark either set by the other wines or lagers. The drinkers didn't stick slavishly to that benchmark but nor did they stray very far.

King Cobra could harness this by adapting their packaging to give more wine cues or by adapting where it's sold. Perhaps placing it in the wine aisle or, even better for the supermarkets, a special section for strong beers in 750ml bottles where a new pricing norm can be established.

How to apply this effect

1. Change your competitive set

Brands should not accept that their 'natural' comparison set is fixed. My experiments show there are sizeable benefits from changing them and the experience of brands, like Red Bull and Nespresso, prove it's possible.

Consider Nespresso. They sell in distinctive pods, which provide the right amount of coffee for a cup. Because they're sold in that unit we compare their price to other places selling by the cup, such as Costa or Caffè Nero. When compared to the £2.50 Costa charge, Nespresso pods, costing 30p–37p, feel like a bargain.

But stop for a second and remember back to when they launched. If Nespresso had sold their coffee in standard packaging the natural comparison set would have been other brands of roast and ground coffee, like Taylor's or illy. Their price would have been judged against the norm for other coffees – roughly £4.00 for 227g. Even with tens of millions of pounds of advertising they could never have persuaded consumers to pay £34 for a 454g bag. But that £34 figure equates to 7p per gram, exactly what they're charging now.

The value of switching comparison sets for Nespresso has been stratospheric. A Bloomberg article estimated their 2015 total annual sales at $4.5bn.

Nespresso is not a one-off. Think about how Red Bull manages to charge such a price premium over other soft drinks. Rory Sutherland, vice Chairman of the Ogilvy & Mather group, says:

> How can Red Bull charge £1.50 a can when Coke only charge 50p? Weirdly you make the can smaller. Suddenly people think this is a different category of drink for which different price points apply. If the can had been the same size, I am not sure they could have charged £1.50. Logic won't tell you that and research won't tell you, because in research we all pretend we are maximisers and hyper-rational.

Or how booze companies sell liquid indistinguishable from a pint but at twice the price, simply by putting it in a bottle.

Unfortunately, not all examples of price relativity are positive for the brand in question. Consider the case of video-conferencing. According to Rory Sutherland:

> Video conferencing has failed to take off, because it is framed as a cheap alternative to something else – air travel. It is like margarine to British Airways' butter... The video conference needs re-framing as the rich man's phone call, not the poor man's air trip. It should be installed in the CEO's office and nowhere else, and certainly not in a basement room.

2. Introduce a higher-end line

A simpler approach than forging a new comparison set is to adapt your own product range. Introducing a higher-end offering establishes a new comparison benchmark and, therefore, makes your other lines seem better value.

An experiment by Amos Tversky and Itamar Simonson in 1993 quantified the effectiveness of this approach. The Stanford University psychologists questioned 221 participants about which camera they would prefer to buy. One group selected between two cameras: the Minolta X-370 priced at $170 or the Minolta Maxxum 3000i at $240. In that scenario roughly 50% chose each option.

The second group were shown three cameras: the original two plus a high-end Minolta Maxxum 7000i, priced at $470. Now, if consumers selected goods on their absolute characteristics the introduction of a new product shouldn't change the ratio of sales between the existing two cameras.

But that's not what happened. The introduction of a high-end option changed the dynamics. The middle option became much more popular – 57% chose it, compared to 22% for the cheapest option.

> Introducing a higher-end offering establishes a new comparison benchmark and, therefore, makes your other lines seem better value.

The preference for the middle option occurs repeatedly. Buyers are often uncertain about what makes for a good product – they worry that the expensive option will be overpriced and the cheapest will be shoddy. The middle option offers protection from these extremes.

Any brand that has a standard and premium range can introduce a third high-end option. This will shift from the cheapest variant to the higher margin, premium one.

For example, a chain of coffee shops could introduce a more expensive blend, a roaster's choice maybe, as well as a highly expensive grand reserve blend.

With this tactic the measurement approach has to be spot on. In the coffee example the success of the approach should be judged by whether sales shift to the high-margin blends. If the grand reserve is introduced and doesn't sell a bean that doesn't matter.

If you're going to use price relativity to shape perceptions of your brand it's best to do so when it launches. This is due to the primacy effect. This is a well-established finding in psychology that the first impressions shape subsequent experiences. We'll investigate the primacy effect in the next chapter.

BIAS 10

Primacy Effect

First impressions shape the subsequent experiences

After choosing your sandwich you remember that you promised to pick up lunch for your colleagues, Tom and Anna. Tom asked for a steak wrap, a bag of crisps and a Coke whereas Anna wanted a cheese baguette and an apple. But what else? You struggle to remember her drink order. You take a gamble and grab a bottle of water. After all, she's always trying to be healthy.

YOUR INABILITY TO remember Anna's drink might be due to the order in which you were told the items. Evidence from Solomon Asch, one of the 20th century's most illustrious psychologists, suggests that the order we hear information affects how it's interpreted.

In a 1946 experiment, Asch, then a teacher at Brooklyn College, described an anonymous person to two groups. The participants in group A were told that the person was intelligent, industrious, impulsive, critical, stubborn and envious. The list started with positive traits, such as intelligence, then moved onto neutral ones, like impulsiveness, and ended with a negative, being envious. In group B the participants heard the same list of attributes but in reverse order: envious, stubborn, critical, impulsive, industrious and intelligent.

Both groups then had to describe the person in their own words. Those who heard the positive characteristics first, were more likely to craft a positive description. For example, one member of that group said:

> The person is intelligent and fortunately he puts his intelligence to work. That he is stubborn and impulsive may be due to the fact that he knows what he is saying and what he means and will not therefore give in easily to someone else's idea which he disagrees with.

In contrast, those hearing the negative statements first tended to be more critical. Again, a quote from one of the participants is illustrative:

> This person's good qualities such as industry and intelligence are bound to be restricted by jealousy and stubbornness. The person is emotional. He is unsuccessful because he is weak and allows his bad points to cover up his good ones.

In Asch's words:

> The impression produced by A is predominantly that of an able person who possesses certain shortcomings which do not, however, overshadow his merits. On the other hand, B impresses the majority as a "problem," whose abilities are hampered by his serious difficulties. Further, some of the qualities (e.g. impulsiveness, criticalness) are interpreted in a positive way under Condition A, while they take on, under Condition B, a negative colour.

Asch's experiment had a quantitative element too. He asked participants what positive characteristics, from a list of 18, they thought the anonymous person might have. The participants in condition A rated the person higher on 14 out of the 18 characteristics. For example, 52% of condition A thought the person would be generous, compared to only 21% among group B.

Asch termed the superior impact of the first information we hear the *primacy effect*.

Still relevant 70 years later?

There are two problems with Asch's experiment from a modern-day marketer's perspective. First, it took place 70 years ago – only a year after the end of World War Two – and, second, it relates to people rather than products.

With that in mind, I told 500 consumers about a fictitious brand, *Black Sheep Vodka*, supposedly launching in the UK soon. Half were told the vodka was: award-winning, refreshing, satisfying, vinegary and weak. The other half were told the same set of adjectives but, as in Asch's experiment, the order was flipped, first weak, then vinegary, satisfying, refreshing and award-winning. When consumers heard the positives first they rated the vodka 11% higher.

Asch's findings apply today.

How to apply this effect

1. Ensure you go first

There are competing explanations for Asch's findings. One theory is that our limited cognitive capacity means that our memory is saturated by the earliest items and our ability to store later information is compromised. This explanation is supported by research from Herman Ebbinghaus, whose work we discussed in the previous chapter. He coined the phrase the serial position effect to describe how the first items that we encounter in a list are more likely to be recalled than the ones in the middle.

If you accept this argument then there are two implications. First, be single-minded in your communications. If your ads contain multiple messages then you risk the consumer's attentional capacity being taken up with the least compelling argument.

Second, if consumers encounter your ad alongside other messages then ensure you're the first message they see, whether that's in a TV break or a magazine. By doing so you boost the probability of being the ad that they remember.

2. Ensure your first impression is as strong as possible

The alternative explanation, favoured by Asch, is that the initial words conjure an image through which subsequent information is filtered. In Asch's words:

> The first terms set up in most subjects a direction which then exerts a continuous effect on the latter terms. When the subject hears the first term, a broad, uncrystallised but directed impression is born. The next characteristic comes not as a separate item, but is related to the established direction. Quickly the view formed acquires a certain stability, so that later characteristics are fitted—if conditions permit— to the given direction.

This explanation leads to different recommendations. The first is that brands might be obsessing too much about the exact characteristics that they communicate. Asch's work suggests that the characteristics we believe brands to have are not held independently. If a brand establishes a strong association with one positive characteristic it will colour other attitudes.

> # If a brand establishes a strong association with one positive characteristic it will colour other attitudes.

This has important implications. It suggests brands should be less concerned about associating themselves with the values rated as most important in a category and instead focus on the values that are easiest to be associated with. Success in building these associations will inadvertently colour other attributes.

Second is the importance of a launch. Asch's experiment showed that first impressions last. Once initial impressions have been formed they're hard to overturn as subsequent impressions are interpreted through them. The same is true when advertisers begin communicating about a new brand. If they generate negative impressions early on then their later communications will struggle to overturn them. Marketers need to invest a disproportionately large proportion of their budget into their launch.

3. Fake brands can be helpful

When I recreated Asch's experiment, I invented a fake brand called *Black Sheep Vodka*. The participants were shown an image of the brand and a small blurb announcing that it was launching in the UK imminently.

I often create fictitious brands for experiments as it makes the research cleaner. If you question participants about a real brand they already have established feelings about it. This means it becomes harder to isolate the effect of the variable that you're testing. Try it for yourself.

When I questioned consumers about *Black Sheep Vodka* they didn't sample the brand. Instead, they predicted the quality of the drink based on a description. These predictions are important as what we taste is influenced by what we expect to taste. That's the focus of the next chapter.

BIAS 11

Expectancy Theory

*How expectations of a product
shape the performance*

On the walk back from the supermarket you wolf down your chicken sandwich and salt and vinegar crisps. All that food makes you feel sluggish so you stop at a café for a flat white. As the weekend is nearly here you decide to treat yourself to their Nicaraguan coffee bean roast. It's 20p more than the standard blend but it tastes so much better that it's well worth the premium.

Does the fancy coffee blend actually taste nicer or is it all in your mind? It's hard to unpick completely but a significant part of the superior taste is due to your higher expectations. You experience what you expect to experience. You expect the coffee to taste better, and, therefore, it does.

THIS ISN'T EMPTY conjecture. Brian Wansink, Professor of Behaviour and Nutritional Science at Cornell University, quantified the effect in 2006 with an experiment at the Bevier Cafeteria in Urbana, Illinois. He told customers that the cafeteria was considering adding a brownie to the menu and they could have a free sample if they answered two simple questions. First, how much would they be prepared to pay for the brownie on their next visit and second, how would they rate the taste?

All in all he gave out 175 brownies: each one the same size, from the same recipe, even with the same powdered sugar dusting. The twist was that unbeknown to the customers they received the brownie in one of three different serving styles: either on snow-white china, a paper plate or a napkin.

Since the brownies were identical any difference in rating or price was due to how they were served. The brownies served on a napkin were rated as "OK", those on a paper plate as "good" and those on china as "excellent". The variations in price were even more striking. Customers were prepared to pay 53c for the brownies on the napkin, 76c on the paper plate and $1.27 on the china. That's a doubling of the price – just by improving the presentation.

From brownies to booze

Brownies are brilliant, but they're not a high-spending ad category. I wanted to test if Wansink's experiments had broader application, in particular among booze brands. Anna Kandasamy, Spencer Corrigan and I toured London offering park-goers lager samples. Drinkers tried the lager in either plastic cups, plain glasses or the appropriate branded glasses. Just as in Wansink's experiment the serving method affected taste: the better the serve, the better the taste.

On a basic level, this provides justification for the millions of pounds invested in glassware. But, as ever, the interesting points were in the nuances. The scale of the effect was in inverse proportion to the size of the brand. If drinkers know the brand well, then the experience of the serve forms just a small part of their knowledge and it has a modest impact. In contrast, when a drink is unknown the serve forms a much greater proportion of the consumer's knowledge and generates a more sizeable effect. Branded glassware is of greater value to smaller brands.

The second finding is that when drinkers disliked the brand then drinking lager out of a branded glass made those associations more salient and damaged the taste.

How to apply this effect

1. Presentation is as important as product

Expectations can generate as much value as the actual product. This leads to multiple opportunities. The most literal is to invest as much time and effort on your brand's physical presentation as your product. Otherwise there's a danger that products won't be appreciated as much as they could be.

Unfortunately, there's a mechanistic mindset which is deeply suspicious of presentation as a source of value. It is best reflected in the Ralph Waldo Emerson's supposed dismissal of such fripperies:

> If a man write a better book, preach a better sermon, or make a better mouse-trap than his neighbour, tho' he build his house in the woods, the world will make a beaten path to his door.

Not true. Far better to listen to Ludwig von Mises, the leading figure in the Austrian School of economics, who said, "If you run a restaurant there is no healthy distinction to be made between the value you create by cooking the food, and the value you create by sweeping the floor".

2. Why good copywriting is like a china plate

The power of presentation is not limited to the physical. Positive sets of expectations can be established through the right image or copy.

Once again Brian Wansink has investigated. In 2005 he quantified the power of tweaking names on menus by undertaking a six-week experiment in a university cafeteria. 'Red Beans with Rice' was renamed 'Cajun Red Beans with Rice', 'Seafood Filet' became 'Succulent Italian Seafood Filet', and 'Chocolate Pudding' was upgraded to 'Satin Chocolate Pudding'. Nothing changed other than the name. Having eaten either the food with the regular labels or the more descriptive ones, 140 students rated the dishes' taste and appeal on a nine-point scale.

The mean score for the plainly described dishes was 6.83 for taste and 5.87 for appeal. In contrast, more descriptive dishes were rated 7.31 for taste and 6.66 for appeal. Detailed descriptions boosted taste and appeal by 7% and 13% respectively.

The label improved the expectation and the expectation improved the taste of the food. Better copywriting had the same effect as serving the food on beautiful china.

3. Unintended consequences

The expectations that brands create are not just the ones that the brand owner intends. Consumers are not passive. They have a whole range of prejudices and biases through which they interpret a brand's communications. This often leads to unintended consequences. Words lovingly chosen to describe a brand may have a specific set of associations in a marketer's mind but another in the consumer's.

> The label improved the expectation and the expectation improved the taste of the food.

Consider green goods. Rebecca Strong and I conducted an experiment to quantify the impact of labelling washing-machine tablets as 'ecologically friendly'.

We sent a group of consumers the same type of washing-machine tablet. They washed a load of clothes and reported back on the tablet's performance. The twist was that half were told that they were testing a standard supermarket tablet, the other half a green variant.

Once again, there was an element of subterfuge. We didn't ask consumers directly what they thought of green goods. Generally, they make positive noises. Instead, we monitored behaviour in test and control conditions.

The results were clear. Those who used the green variant rated the tablet as worse on all metrics.

Respondents scored the eco tablet 9% lower for both effectiveness and likeability, while the number who would recommend the product was 11% lower and the number who would buy it themselves, 18% lower than for the standard version.

Despite eco-friendly products often having a higher price, consumers who tested the green tablet were only prepared to pay £4.41 on average compared to £4.82 for the standard version. Consumers believe that products involve a trade-off: improved eco-friendliness entails corresponding loss in cleaning efficacy. This is a concern for any brand interested in a green variant. If brands in this category are going to successfully sell green variants, they'll need to counteract these negative associations, or spend heavily to bolster their cleaning credentials.

There is a broader application, beyond green goods. You need to investigate the set of expectations associated with your positioning. Sugar free, low alcohol, eco-friendly. These areas might be wholly positive in your mind but what do consumers think? A series of test and control experiments like the one Rebecca and I undertook should help flush them out before you undertake an expensive launch.

Unfortunately, persuading consumers that their assumptions about green goods or low-alcohol beer are wrong is a tough task. Once an idea has taken hold it's remarkably hard to shift. That's due to confirmation bias. In the next chapter, I'll discuss this problem and what you can do to avoid it...

BIAS 12

Confirmation Bias

Its danger and how to avoid it

> You can hear Eva, one of your colleagues, before you see her. She's going round the office jauntily shaking a collection tin. Eva's drumming up sponsors for a marathon she's running. Your colleagues are impressed by her altruism. But you're not fooled, not for a second. It's an obvious ploy to win popularity.

YOU'RE DISPLAYING SIGNS of confirmation bias. Because Eva was promoted ahead of you, you're cynical about her motivations, interpreting them through a lens of your existing feelings.

The evidence for confirmation bias stretches back to the experiments of Albert Hastorf and Hadley Cantril. The psychologists based their findings on an American football game between stark rivals: Princeton and Dartmouth University. In the psychologists' turn of phrase, the game was full of "rough play". Quite an understatement: the Princeton quarterback broke his nose and the Dartmouth quarterback broke a leg.

In the bitter aftermath the academics showed footage of the game to 324 Princeton and Dartmouth students and asked them to count the number of fouls committed by each side. The results were conclusive. Students were twice as likely to see the opposition commit a foul as they were to spot a foul by their own team. The match was seen through a prism of loyalty.

In politics as in football

The experiment is not an historical anomaly. In 2015, during the UK general election, Jenny Riddell and I surveyed 1,004 nationally representative voters about their views on raising VAT by a penny to fund 10,000 extra nurses. The results were then split by political affiliation. The twist was that half the respondents were told it was a Conservative policy and half were told it was an initiative by Labour.

When Labour supporters thought the policy came from their party there was strong support: 14% completely agreed. However, support plummeted to 3%, less than a quarter of the original level, when it was described as a Conservative proposal. Similarly, among Tories the policy was four times more popular when it was seen to come from their party. The scale of the effect means that policy is far less influential than existing party affiliation.

Why is this relevant for you?

The experiments prove that it's hard to overturn negative opinions. Rejecters of your brand are difficult to convince because they interpret your message through a lens of negativity.

As the legendary stock market investor, Charlie Munger, said:

> The human mind is a lot like the human egg, in that the human egg has a shut-off device. One sperm gets in, and it shuts down so that the next one can't get in. The human mind has a big tendency of the same sort.

How to apply this effect

1. Identify who it's best to target

On a finite budget, focus your money where it makes the biggest impact. That means avoiding rejecters. I term this process "marketing triage", after the medical procedure devised by Dominique Jean Larrey, chief surgeon in Napoleon's army. He ordered his surgeons to split incoming patients into three categories (hence the word triage, from the French, 'to sort out'):

1. Those likely to live regardless of the care they receive.

2. Those unlikely to live regardless of the care they receive.

3. And finally, those for whom immediate care might make a difference.

In a similar vein, marketers should apply a threefold categorisation of their own:

1. Those likely to buy regardless of communications.

2. Those unlikely to buy regardless of communications.

3. And those for whom communications might make a difference.

Marketing efforts should ruthlessly focus on the final category. This sounds blindingly obvious, but from my own work with brands I've rarely seen it applied.

The reason to avoid rejecters is sound though – confirmation bias means it requires inordinate efforts to convince them.

Similarly, ignore heavy buyers. Their purchase frequency means they are routinely exposed to the brand's packaging, website and store. These touchpoints therefore become disproportionately important in shaping perceptions. Additionally, Byron Sharp's work shows that heavy buyers offer limited headroom. If you're already buying a can of Coca-Cola a day, how much more can you polish off? Finally, these customers will be far more interested in your ads than average, so they'll overhear campaigns aimed at other people anyway.

By focusing on the lukewarm, spend is targeted to where it works best. This means that more brands will be able to afford a constant presence.

2. Identify when to talk to rejecters

Of course, there are rare occasions when you can't avoid rejecters. Perhaps they're such a large or vocal group that ignoring them jeopardises your future. In this scenario, the solution is to target them when they're distracted.

Counter-intuitive? Maybe, but the supporting evidence originates from one of the 20th century's greatest psychologists: Leon Festinger.

In 1964, Festinger and Nathan Maccoby, academics at Stanford University, recruited members of college fraternities. They played those students an audio argument about why fraternities were morally wrong. The recording was played in two different scenarios: students either heard it on its own or they watched a silent film at the same time.

After the students had heard the recording, the Stanford psychologists questioned them as to how far their views had shifted. Those who had heard the argument at the same time as the silent film were more likely to have changed their opinion.

We're more easily persuaded when focusing on more than one thing at a time.

The psychologists' hypothesis was that the brain is adept at generating counter-arguments that maintain its existing opinions, but when the brain is distracted that ability is hampered. We're more easily persuaded when focusing on more than one thing at a time.

The lesson is clear: target rejecters when they're partially distracted. Luckily, these moments are becoming more common. As Herbert Simon, who won the Nobel Prize for Economics in 1978, pointed out, we live in an information rich age and:

what information consumes is rather obvious: it consumes the attention of its recipients. Hence a wealth of information creates a poverty of attention.

It's your task to pinpoint these moments of inattention. When targeting rejecters, brands should prioritise media such as radio, which tend to be consumed while people are doing something else.

Even with a medium like TV, which is often the sole focus of attention, media planners can identify the programmes or times when the audience is likely to be second screening. According to Nielsen's global AdReaction study, among people with access to multiple devices, an average of 35% of TV viewing time was spent simultaneously watching TV and using another device. The best programmes to reach second screeners are either those with a social nature, *Made in Chelsea* being a prime example, or low involvement, such as daytime TV.

One of the most cherished beliefs of media planners, that attention is crucial, may not be right in all circumstances. This is particularly interesting when you bear in mind the hefty premium for attentive moments. For example, cinema ads, perhaps the medium that gets the highest attention, trade at a five times the cost of TV. By targeting distraction you benefit twice. First, you're more likely to overturn misconceptions and second you pay less for the pleasure.

3. How to win over rejecters

As the brain can generate counter-arguments prolifically when directly challenged, it's best to avoid this. Instead use subtler cues. That way the conscious mind doesn't realise it's being persuaded and confirmation bias isn't activated.

The British Airways ads illustrate the pervasive power of subtle cues – ever since 1989 they have featured the *Flower Duet* from Delibes' opera *Lakmé* as the soundtrack. If British Airways had directly claimed they were luxurious, Festinger's theory suggests consumers would scour their memories for counter-arguments. However, since this isn't explicitly stated, the brain's capability isn't activated. Instead, the beautiful strains of the *Flower Duet* insinuate luxury by association.

Advertisers, therefore, have two options. The recommended route is to apply the process of marketing triage and avoid targeting rejecters and heavy buyers.

A riskier alternative is to convert this resistant audience by reaching them at moments of distraction or with oblique and incidental detail. Whether that turns out to be brave or foolhardy depends on the execution.

Another reason why entrenched opinions are so hard to shift is that most people are overly confident in their abilities. Since people tend to think they're cleverer than average there's a tendency to ignore contrary opinions from other people. The bias of overconfidence is the subject of the next chapter.

BIAS 13

Overconfidence

A bias that afflicts marketers and consumers alike

You receive an email from your boss scheduling your annual review for next week. In preparation, you start making notes about this year's successful projects. In your opinion, it's an impressive list. Perhaps you should push harder this year for a pay rise? After all you're much better at your job than most of your colleagues.

YOU ARE NOT alone in believing that you're above average. Most people do. This tendency has been studied by David Dunning and Justin Kruger, and the inspiration for their experiment is my favourite story in psychology.

On 19 April 1995, McArthur Wheeler robbed two Pittsburgh banks and, unfortunately for him, was caught in a matter of hours. Why such fast capture? Wheeler had robbed both banks in broad daylight, without a mask. There must have been plenty of witnesses. But what led him to attempt such a brazen, foolhardy crime? He mistakenly believed that his face was invisible – because he had rubbed it with lemon juice. As far as he was concerned, if it works for invisible ink, why not skin?

This tale of comic incompetence perturbed Dunning and Kruger.

How could this robber think that he had the ability to evade capture?

It made them ponder whether misplaced confidence was commonplace – if not quite so extreme. To test this, the researchers recruited 194 students to take a series of logic and grammar tests and then asked them to predict how they compared to their peers.

Just like Wheeler, though perhaps not to the same farcical extent, participants were poor judges of performance and they systematically overestimated their ability. For example, in the grammar tests, participants estimated they were in the 68th percentile: better than two-thirds of other students. The discrepancy between estimates and reality was starkest among the weakest students. The worst quarter of students estimated that they were in the 61st percentile.

Overconfidence occurs in many situations. In 1981 Ola Svenson, a psychologist at the University of Stockholm, found that 88% of drivers believed they were safer than average. The bias even afflicts the very people who should be aware of it: a 1977 study by K. Patricia Cross found that more than 90% of academics at the University of Nebraska thought they were better than average at teaching.

How to apply this effect

1. Beware overconfidence

The point of the academic studies is not to laugh at the folly of others. Overconfidence affects us all. To quantify the scale of the problem within marketing, I conducted an experiment. I surveyed 117 agency staff and, among other questions, I asked them how good they were at their job compared to their peers: 83% claimed they were better than average. This is not a one-off. I have run this experiment three times and on each occasion, I've had the same results.

Overconfidence in marketers is not harmless: I've identified two repercussions.

First, in budget setting. If you think your next piece of creative will outshine the competition, then the temptation is to spend less than your rivals on media. After all, stronger creative achieves the same impact as mediocre creative but on smaller budgets. The potential media savings can be significant.

The temptation to scrimp on your budget should be resisted. The odds are that your next campaign will be of average quality. (If you disagree please re-read the beginning of this chapter.) If you set a relatively light budget, you're hampering your chances of success.

Second, there is the problem of prematurely jettisoning successful ad campaigns. Many brilliant campaigns, far superior to the competition, eventually lose their lustre. They still outperform the competition but not to the same degree as they did in their heyday. This is when discussions about a new creative route often start.

> ## If you have an above average campaign, it's best not to muck around with it.

I witnessed this first-hand on two campaigns: 118 118 and the Halifax. The two brands had extraordinarily strong campaigns in the early 2000s: Halifax with their singing bank manager, Howard, and 118 118 with their runners. Both won gold at the IPA Effectiveness awards. But over time the effectiveness declined. Even though the creative still outperformed rivals, the marketing teams were convinced that they could emulate the original success with a new creative direction. Both brands were disappointed. The new campaigns were distinctly average.

If you have an above average campaign, it's best not to muck around with it. In Rory Sutherland's words:

> Can you point to a single brand which has really suffered because it has stuck with the same strategy and creative approach for too long? Because it changed tack too rarely? Because it retained an old endline?

2. The problem of overconfidence is growing

Marketers have more data about consumers than ever before. While most marketers welcome this torrent of information, there is a downside. It exacerbates overconfidence.

The problem of more data was investigated by Paul Slovic, Professor of Psychology at the University of Oregon. He ran an experiment with professional horseracing handicap setters in which they were given a list of 88 variables that were useful in predicting a horse's performance. The participants then had to predict the outcome of the race and their confidence in their prediction. They repeated these tasks with access to different levels of data: either 5, 10, 20, 30 or 40 of the variables.

> # We shouldn't harness data just because we can.

The results were illuminating. Accuracy was the same regardless of the number of variables used. However, overconfidence grew as more data was harnessed. Experts overestimated the importance of factors that had a limited value. It was only when five data points were used that accuracy and confidence were well calibrated.

Marketers face a similar set of problems. They have access to more data than ever before and many believe that because the information exists they should use it. The Slovic experiment suggests otherwise. We shouldn't harness data just because we can. Instead, as much time should be spent choosing which data sets to ignore as which to use.

3. Turn consumer overconfidence to your advantage

Overconfidence isn't limited to those working in marketing: it also occurs among the public, which represents an opportunity. Since most people believe they are above average, a brand that communicates typical behaviour could encourage people to surpass that benchmark.

Take charitable donations. When I surveyed 521 people I found that 64% believed they were more generous than their peers. If charities communicated the average donation level to potential donors, it would encourage them to exceed that amount. Unless donors gave a higher amount, how could they continue to think of themselves as so generous?

One danger of overconfidence is that we're too certain in our beliefs. This means that we fail to question them enough and therefore that we hold onto flawed ideas for too long. We'll investigate one such flawed marketing belief, brand purpose, in the next chapter.

BIAS 14

Wishful Seeing

*What we see is sometimes
what we want to see*

Your team have spent the last week working hard preparing for a pitch. As their energy seems to be flagging, you decide on a whim to pop out and buy them some treats. You walk back to the supermarket you went to for lunch. As you are mulling over what sweets would be most popular, you spot a crumpled fiver on the pavement ahead.

You break into a half-jog, half-run to get there before anyone else. However, as you stoop down to grab it you realise that you were mistaken. It's just a flyer.

THE IDEA THAT what we perceive is not an objective reflection of the physical world stretches back to the 1940s and the New Look school of psychology.

Jerome Bruner and Cecile Goodman, psychologists at Harvard University, ran an experiment in 1947 that suggested that what we saw partly reflected our desires. They showed children five denominations of coins, one at a time. After each one the children had to adjust a projector until the beam of light was the same size as the coin. The experimenters then repeated the process with a separate group of children, but this time using gray cardboard discs the same dimensions as the coins.

The children who had seen the cardboard discs overestimated the size by a fraction, a mere 1.4% on average. In contrast, those who had seen coins overestimated their size by 27%. The psychologists inferred that the children's desire for the coins made them loom larger.

Their supposition was confirmed by two additional findings. First, the scale of the exaggeration broadly increased as the coins became more valuable. So, for example, the children misjudged the penny by just 17% but the dime by a whopping 29%.

The clincher though came when they split the data by the wealth of the children. They had recruited half the children from Boston slums and half from prosperous neighbourhoods. The poor children overestimated the coins by 37%, more than twice the rate of the rich children who exaggerated the size by 17%. Their hypothesis was that since money meant more to the poorer children they exaggerated the size of coins further.

In the years since the experiment psychologists have come to accept that people don't passively record reality. They term the behaviour *wishful seeing*.

How wishful seeing explains marketing's infatuation with brand purpose

Wishful seeing has profound implications for the business of advertising. Agencies have been guilty of promoting theories of advertising that they want to be true, rather than ones that actually are true. And there is no better example of this than brand ideals or purpose.

Over the last five years brand purpose, the idea that brands which have a purpose beyond profit outperform those that don't, has become one of the most widely promoted ideas in advertising. Professor

Mark Ritson, the outspoken columnist at *Marketing Week*, calls it a "discipline shredding claim".

The evidence supporting brand purpose comes from *Grow*, a book written by Jim Stengel, ex-CMO of P&G. Stengel came up with this finding after selecting the 50 brands with the highest loyalty or bonding scores from Millward Brown's 50,000-strong database. These star performers were termed the Stengel 50. Stengel then searched for a link between the brands. This was found to be a *Brand Ideal* – a shared intent by everyone in the business to improve people's lives.

Next he looked at the chosen brands' stock value growth between 2000 and 2011. Since the Stengel 50 had grown by 393% compared with a 7% loss for the S&P 500 benchmark, he declared that ideals were driving business success. Ideals supposedly didn't just drive growth; they led to stratospheric success.

The book has had a tremendous impact. Martin Sorrell, CEO of WPP, declared he was "utterly convinced". Tom Peters, the management guru, was even more impressed, calling the book a "landmark". Part of its appeal is that it offers a simple recipe for success: an off-the-shelf solution that works regardless of the nuances of the brand or category. That's an enticing prospect for time-pressed managers grappling with uncertainty. But there's more to it than that. It also imbues advertising with a moral purpose, an appealing prospect for those hankering for a deeper meaning to their careers.

However, because advertisers fervently hoped that the theory was true, they forgot to check whether it was. They have succumbed to a collective bout of wishful seeing.

How to apply this effect

1. Don't assume brand purpose will solve your marketing problems

Before you search for a purpose for your brand you should scrutinise Stengel's findings. I propose four tests:

1. The experimental data is accurate.

2. The tactic predicts the future, not just the past.

3. The brands that outperform the stock market are linked by an ideal.

4. Those brands with ideals outperform those without.

Let's look at those tests in some more detail.

1) Is the data accurate?

A basic requirement is that the data being analysed is accurate. Stengel's central piece of data is that his 50 stocks rose by 393%. But that's not quite the case. Some of the companies in question, such as Emirates and Wegmans, are privately held, which means they don't have a share price.

Nor do other brands in the Stengel 50, like Stonyfield Farm, Innocent or Pampers, have a share price. They are parts of much larger publicly-traded companies, respectively Danone, Coca-Cola and P&G. In Stonyfield Farm's case its 2014 revenues were less than 2% of Danone's. Can you claim that Danone's share price rose because 2% of its holdings have a brand ideal?

The gravest flaw though is how Stengel selected the 50 brands. He picked the best performers in Millward Brown's 50,000-strong database. That's the top 0.1% of brands. It's not surprising that those brands performed well in terms of share price. If they hadn't performed well in the past they wouldn't be in Millward Brown's top 0.1% of brands.

Stengel's finding, if you re-state it at its most basic, is that brands that feature in the top 0.1% of companies have performed well in the stock market. That's circular logic.

2) Does the theory predict the future as well as the past?

The true test of a theory is if it accurately predicts the future. With that in mind I examined the share price performance of 26 of Stengel's companies over the five years up to March 2017. Since this is after the publication of his book, it tests the predictive ability of the theory. Remember I'm analysing 26 companies, as it's misleading to include brands who account for a small proportion of a larger company's incomes.

The results?

A mere 9 of the 26 companies studied outperformed the S&P 500 benchmark. By chance alone you'd expect half, or 13, of the stocks to exceed that benchmark. This suggests that ideals weren't the panacea Stengel suggested.

3) Are the brands linked by an ideal?

For the theory to be valid the brands in question must be linked by an ideal. Unfortunately, even this doesn't seem to be true.

The claim that all 50 of the brands exhibit an ideal is suspicious. Theories rarely predict events so conveniently; reality is messier. The reason Stengel claims such widespread uptake of ideals becomes apparent when you examine his definitions. He stretches the term *ideal* to such an extent that it's meaningless.

Have a look at his definition for three of the brands:

→ Moët & Chandon – "exists to transform occasions into celebrations".

→ Mercedes-Benz – "exists to epitomise a life of achievement".

→ BlackBerry – "exists to connect people with one another and the content that is most important in their lives, anytime, anywhere".

Notice a problem? These ideals are just category descriptors. They could apply to any champagne, luxury brand or handset provider.

This isn't a subjective opinion. In 2015 Aidan O'Callaghan and I asked 1,000 consumers to match one of six brands to each of these ideals. If the ideals were a genuine fit, you'd expect consumers to recognise his brands. Yet only 6%, 10% and 21% of those questioned recognised BlackBerry, Mercedes and Moët respectively.

If the term ideal can cover anything, then it's meaningless.

4) Do brands with ideals outperform those that don't?

In order to prove that ideals enable success you must compare successful brands with unsuccessful ones. In particular, you must demonstrate that successful companies are more likely to have taken ideals to their heart. You can't make sweeping claims by looking at a single group in isolation. Otherwise you might attribute success to an inconsequential factor common to all brands.

Unfortunately, Stengel makes no attempt to determine whether brands outside the top 50 have an absence of ideals. This alone means his case is unproven.

In the interest of trying to prove Stengel's theory, I examined some of the worst stock market performers of recent times. Consider Nokia, whose shares plummeted 95% between October 2007 and July 2012. One could claim that, like BlackBerry, it existed "to connect people with one another and the content that is most important in their lives, anytime, anywhere". This isn't just my opinion. The consumers O'Callaghan and I surveyed were 52% more likely to think Nokia fitted this ideal than BlackBerry. It seems ideals apply as much to underperforming brands as successful ones.

How does Stengel's theory fare against our tests?

Stengel claims to have found the secret to business growth. If true he would have fundamentally changed how brands should advertise. But such a sweeping assertion requires robust evidence. As Carl Sagan, the American astronomer argued, "Extraordinary claims require extraordinary evidence". Stengel provides neither ordinary nor extraordinary evidence.

Unfortunately, Stengel's work has failed all four of the required tests. Stengel has failed to prove that ideals drive superior profits.

But this failure raises another question:

If brand purpose is so flawed why are marketers keen to adopt it?

I travelled to Old Street to find out. Vic Polkinghorne, co-founder and Creative Director of Sell! Sell!, is one of advertising's most vocal critics of brand purpose. He suggests that its popularity is due to the motivations of marketers rather than what's beneficial for the brand in question.

According to Polkinghorne:

> It comes down to people, because this is a people business. I think it's about how people view themselves and how they spend their time. (Ad folk) want to feel good about themselves. That's perfectly understandable. It's not wrong for people to want to feel good about themselves. The problem is that some people don't feel rewarded by helping a company be more successful at selling products. They therefore look for something more from their work.

Marketers bought into the ideal mythology because they wanted it to be true. As Shakespeare had Julius Caesar say: "men may construe things after their fashion/clean from the purpose of the things themselves".

2. Be sceptical about anyone who claims to have a universal key to success

Stengel has failed in his stated objective of proving the value of brand purpose. But there's a deeper flaw in his work: his attempt to find a universal approach for ad campaigns. The idea of a marketing approach that works in all situations is flawed. Brands operate in too varied a range of situations. Advertising campaigns cover everything from a granny tacking up a lost cat poster to a tree, to a corporate behemoth lobbying the government to change policy. How can a single approach be right in such a range of situations? What succeeds in one context might flop in another time or place.

> # The idea of a marketing approach that works in all situations is flawed.

Polkinghorne states:

> It's like everything in this business. The answer might sometimes be yes and sometimes it might be no. It just depends on the category and the situation. I get really concerned about people who have a simple answer to everything.

Hunting for a guaranteed formula for success is a fool's errand. As Phil Rosenzweig, Professor of Strategy and International Business at IMD, wrote in *The Halo Effect*:

> Anyone who claims to have found laws of business physics either understands little about business, little about physics or little about both.

Second, success is not determined solely by a company's actions. Rosenzweig continues:

> Following a given formula can't ensure high performance, and for a simple reason: in a competitive market economy, performance is fundamentally relative, not absolute. Success

and failure depend not only on a company's actions but also on those of its rivals.

Many well-managed companies fail not for internal reasons, but because of a radical disruption from a competitor. Think of mainframe computers disrupted by PCs or video rental stores bankrupted by streaming services. The destruction of these companies was not due to a lack of purpose. If business performance is impacted by competitors, as surely it must be, then success can never be guaranteed by just sticking to an internal behaviour, like a brand ideal.

But that's enough about the biases that affect advertisers. Let's get back to our main focus, consumers. In particular, how the media context that an ad appears in affects its interpretation.

BIAS 15

Media Context

How the placement of an ad affects its interpretation

You save the presentation that you have been working on intermittently this morning onto a memory stick. The presentation is for a meeting with your largest billing client so you need your boss's approval. You head up to her office on the seventh floor but as her meeting is overrunning you wait outside. There's a pile of fashion magazines on the coffee table in the waiting room so you flick through one, marvelling at the flashy jewellery ads.

THE JEWELLERY ADS in the magazine look impressive partly because of the imagery but also because of the media context. The sheer power of context can be simply illustrated by a visual illusion. Look at the words below.

THE CAT

The text appears to read, 'THE CAT'.

But examine it closely. The 'H' in 'THE' and the 'A' in 'CAT' are identical. We assume that they're different letters because of the context. We've read the words 'THE' and 'CAT' so many times that we presume we know what will appear in the middle. The context shapes the information.

Visual illusions illuminate our thought process. Just as context influences what our eyes see, so it determines what our minds think.

The power of context in media

As with visual illusions, context can determine how messages are interpreted in media.

An experiment by Michael Deppe and his colleagues from the University of Münster, quantified the importance of the media context. In 2005, the neurologists showed 21 consumers 30 news headlines. The respondents rated the believability of the headlines on a seven-point scale, with one being the most credible and seven the least.

The headlines appeared to come from one of four news magazines. Each headline was randomly rotated between the magazines so that each viewer saw the headlines in the context of every magazine. This allowed the researchers to assess the effect of the context on the credibility of the headlines.

The scores were significantly influenced by the magazine. Headlines in the most respected magazine scored on average 1.9, compared to 5.5 in the least regarded magazine.

Information is not processed neutrally. We are swayed by contextual cues.

Jeremy Bullmore, former Creative Director and Chairman of JWT in London, notes that this affects not just headlines, but advertising too:

A small ad reading "Ex-governess seeks occasional evening work" would go largely unremarked in the chaste personal columns of

The Lady. Exactly the same words in the window of a King's Cross newsagent would prompt different expectations.

How to apply this effect

1. The right audience is not enough

Media context is a pertinent topic because of the growth of programmatic advertising.

Programmatic advertising, the automated purchasing of digital advertising, is one of the biggest growth areas in advertising. According to eMarketer, £2.7bn was spent on programmatic digital display in the UK in 2016, up 44% on the previous year.

One of the main components of programmatic advertising is real-time bidding. This enables advertisers to harness the wealth of digital data and make bids on individual ad impressions. This has meant advertisers can now reach specific audiences outside of relevant environments.

Take car buyers (or CEOs). A few years ago, the places where you could reach this audience were limited. Because supply was curtailed, sites like What Car or Top Gear charged a premium. However, once car buyers became identifiable by their cookies, and you could bid on an impression-by-impression level, then you could reach them on any site they visited. Since the supply of sites where you can reach car buyers has ballooned then the price to reach them in non-relevant environments dropped.

Many brands now reach their audiences with little consideration for context. However, Deppe's experiment shows that context affects perceptions. It suggests that all exposures, even in the same medium, can't be valued equally. A message in a highly respected title will gain credibility from the environment.

Of course, while context shapes perception, it does not create it entirely. Look again at "THE CAT". No amount of contextual effect would make you think the "T" was a "C". Context has a subtle, marginal effect.

It might be that the lower prices available in less respected contexts are worthwhile. However, that is a careful calculation. Currently that trade-off is being ignored. We need to factor in the value of context or risk gradually diminishing the brands we're meant to be protecting.

2. The importance of waste

John Kay, an economist at Oxford University, argues that advertising doesn't work because of explicit messages. He suggests that one context is particularly important, that of waste. By waste he means spending more on adverts than is necessary to functionally communicate the explicit message. That could be a 90-second ad, acres of white space on a double-page spread or extravagant production values.

> We need to factor in the value of context or risk gradually diminishing the brands.

Advertising known to be expensive signals the volume of the resources available to the advertiser. As Kay says in his landmark paper:

> The advertiser has either persuaded lots or people to buy his product already, a good sign, or has persuaded someone to lend him lots of money to finance the campaign.

Advertising works, not despite its perceived wastage, but because of it.

Kay further states that since advertising tends to recoup its costs in the long term, only a company with substantial commitment to their brand would invest significant sums of money in advertising. A poor quality brand can advertise to generate trial, but no amount of spend can deliver repeat purchase to disgruntled customers.

In his words, extravagant advertising, therefore, acts as a screening mechanism that:

convincingly signals the quality of a product by displaying the producer's sincere faith in his own output, reflected by the money spent promoting it.

Or, as the ad blogger and author Bob Hoffman puts it more punchily:

Their subconscious logic (is that an oxymoron?) goes something like this: A quality brand has a reputation built over years and worth billions. As a result, they have sufficient resources to advertise in proper places and with a set of skills that is unavailable to less successful, less reliable companies.

They know how and where quality brands advertise and what advertising for quality brands feels like. And they also know where shitty brands advertise.

This theory neatly explains why famous sponsorships are effective. The context demonstrates a costly and, therefore, honest belief in the strength of the advertised product.

Of course, this theory assumes consumers know the price of sponsorships.

Is this the case?

I surveyed 333 consumers about the cost of the Real Madrid shirt sponsorship to find out. Among those who gave a figure, 89% thought it cost more than £30m per year – which is indeed the rough cost.

The power of media context does not have to be as dramatic as a multi-million-pound sponsorship. There are different contextual cues given off by different forms of audio-visual advertising.

I asked 502 people how much they thought advertising on TV, cinema and YouTube cost. The median estimate was £25,000 for a million views of a 30-second ad on cinema and TV but only £5,000 on YouTube. Of course, their guesses might be wrong. But that's irrelevant. What matters is the perception.

Brands must recognise that much of advertising's impact comes from perceived waste. There is a role for bold brand statements, even in an era obsessed with efficiency.

The occasional extravagance displays a confidence that mere ad claims cannot emulate.

Unfortunately, many brand managers struggle to recognise the importance of media context. Part of the reason is they fail to empathise with the consumer experience. The following chapter, called the curse of knowledge, will investigate this in more depth.

BIAS 16

The Curse of Knowledge

How we struggle to empathise with consumers

As you stroll back to your desk you hum contentedly. Norm, a colleague from accounts, stops you in the corridor and asks what you're humming. You hum slower and louder; a wonderful rendition of Bohemian Rhapsody. Norm stares blankly. Tutting, you walk off, he's obviously playing dumb.

You're falling victim to the curse of knowledge – the difficulty of imagining what it's like not to know something that we know.

This problem was demonstrated in 1990 by Elizabeth Newton, a psychologist at Stanford University. She split participants into two groups: *tappers* and *listeners*. The first group chose a song and then, without revealing its name, they tapped out the rhythm for the listeners to guess. The tappers estimated the probability of the song being recognised at 50%. They were wildly wrong. Of the 120 songs in the experiment only 2.5% were identified correctly.

States of mind

What causes the gap between prediction and reality? Well, when the tapper beats out their tune they can't help but hear the song play through their head. However, all the listener hears, in the words of the psychologist Chip Heath, "is a bunch of disconnected taps, like a kind of bizarre Morse Code".

It's hard for the tapper to recreate the state of mind of the listener. The curse of knowledge identified by this experiment creates problems in two distinct areas: design and messaging. Let's turn to the design problem first.

Ad design suffers because the way brand managers approve ads is at odds with how consumers experience them. When weighing up what piece of copy to run, the brand manager tends to pore over the ad, scrutinising each element of the copy, applying their full attention for a considerable length of time to ensure it hits the objectives.

And the consumer?

A cursory glance at the poster as their car speeds by, a fleeting glimpse of a press ad while they flick from page to page, or the barest registration of a banner in their peripheral vision. This disconnect leads to ads that often don't work.

How big a problem is this?

Ifan Batey and I designed a small, informal experiment to quantify the problem. He walked around London's West End and categorised the legibility of all the posters he passed from the other side of the street. He found that 4% were illegible and for more than a third, only the headline could be easily read. This represents a significant waste of money.

Or consider digital display ads, which often follow the rules of print copy. They assume the luxury of a few seconds to snare a reader's attention. Data from Lumen suggests this is not the case. Lumen has a panel of 300 households who have agreed to have eye-tracking sensors installed on their laptops. This allows the research agency to track how long digital ads are looked at during natural browsing. Their data shows that online ads are on average glanced at for only 0.9 seconds. Only 4% of viewers glance at online ads for more than two seconds. Better to think of display space like a poster and keep messages simple.

How to apply this effect

1. Force yourself to be a listener not a maker

I met with Ian Leslie, author of *Born Liars*, in an Indian café near Liverpool Street. Over a bacon naan he pointed out that it wasn't just advertisers who struggle to put themselves in the shoes of their audience. The same difficulties beset musicians.

According to the musician Brian Eno:

> You're a completely different person as a maker than you are as a listener. That's one of the reasons I so often leave the studio to listen to things. A lot of people never leave the studio when they're making something, so they're always in that maker mode, screwdriving things in – adding, adding, adding. Because it seems like the right thing to be doing in that room. But it's when you come out that you start to hear what you like.

Marketers need to adopt Eno's approach and force themselves to change the context of evaluation. If you evaluate the effectiveness of a poster in the offices of the creative agency you'll be in *maker mode*, it's preferable to instead get out onto the street and judge the copy on an actual billboard.

Get out onto the street and judge the copy on an actual billboard.

Even better, monitor consumers' responses using excellent mock-up tools like Posterscope and JCDecaux's 'Virtuocity'.

2. Find out if your audience are maximisers or satisficers

The second issue is one of understanding what messaging will most motivate consumers. Marketers have a substantially deeper relationship with their brand than any sane consumer. An Andrex marketer thinks about toilet rolls for forty hours a week – more time than the buyer will spend in their entire life.

> Striving to convey perfection often leads to a focus on intricate detail irrelevant to most.

In the language of Carnegie Mellon psychologist, Herbert Simon, marketers tend to be maximisers while consumers are most often satisficers. Maximiser describes people who spend considerable time and effort finding the ideal product in a particular category. Satisficers are those who will settle for the first product that meets their criteria.

As Rory Sutherland puts it:

> The vast bulk of the money in any market at any time is in the hands of the satisficers. People who want to meld with a peer group, not to outdo it, and people who are more eager to avoid social embarrassment or regret – including purchase mistakes – than they are to display dominance.

This divergence is only an issue if marketers project their beliefs, attitudes and behaviours onto their customers. When I questioned my colleagues, most denied assuming that their target audience thought like them. Others might make that mistake, but not them – they were professionals.

I needed more relevant proof to sway them. So I sent all my colleagues, and many of our clients, a short survey. The survey included two seemingly innocuous questions: what percentage of the population do you think owns an iPhone and do you own one yourself?

The results were significant. Those who had an iPhone thought half the population owned one, whereas those who didn't thought only a third did. Powerful proof that biases affect marketers just as much as consumers.

Relying on intuition is dangerous – it leads to plans that would influence us but not necessarily the consumer. Maximisers want to know that their product is perfect; satisificers want reassurance it won't be rubbish. Striving to convey perfection often leads to a focus on intricate detail irrelevant to most. In contrast, reassurance comes from stressing the popularity of a brand, whether directly or by investing in high profile, seemingly wasteful displays of advertising that only the most profitable companies can afford.

Brands need to decide whether their audience are maximisers or satisficers and communicate accordingly.

3. Think like a consumer

Another solution is more insight work. Most of us agree with this in principle, but in practice it happens too rarely as it's perceived as devilishly expensive. But insights spring from simple techniques as well as complex ones whether that's interviewing consumers in their homes, spending a day listening in at a call centre, or working in-store for a week.

The ideal solution is to create a bespoke technique for the problem in hand. For example, when working on a brief for a male incontinence brand I wanted to help the agency team involved understand the target audience. We had no budget for this so we used a technique we call *method planning*.

Over a weekend I texted the planners at random times. Each time they received a text they had to stop what they were doing and get to a toilet within two minutes. This helped the planners understand the experience of the target audience. From this experiment we discovered two useful insights. First, incontinence is a minor concern when people are at home. After all, a toilet is a few seconds away. It's when they're away from home that it's a worry. This led us to recommend media which reached people at the maximum moment of concern, such as tube car panels.

Second, our participants mentioned that while the experiment was inconvenient for them, it was also a burden on their families. This led us to the insight that maybe it was better to encourage older, male sufferers to rectify the issue not for their benefit, but for their family's.

And the cost of all this? About 50p on my phone bill.

Insight work doesn't need to be expensive and it doesn't need to be complex. There's no excuse not to better understand the buyer.

However, not all tracking data helps you better understand your audience. Sometimes data can be downright misleading if not interpreted correctly. We'll address that issue in the next chapter.

BIAS 17

Goodhart's Law

The danger of poorly set digital targets

Today is the last working day of the quarter and you need to register a large sale to hit your target. If you manage, you'll receive your bonus. That should be simple, as one of your longest-standing clients has promised to place an order today.

However, when you ring to confirm sign-off, the client is busy and wants to complete the paperwork on Monday. You panic and offer her a 10%, then a 25% and, finally, a 50% discount if the sale can be authorised immediately. The client agrees. But at the end of the call she wonders whether the previous prices were inflated? You mumble an unconvincing answer...

YOU COULD HAVE doubled your company's income from the sale by waiting, but that would have jeopardised your bonus. From your perspective this was a rational decision, but it's counter to your employer's intention. They created the bonus system to boost income, but in this case it has reduced it.

This poorly set target, which led to unintended consequences, is an example of *Goodhart's Law*. This states:

When a measure becomes a target, it ceases to be a good measure.

One infamous example of unintended consequences is from Hanoi, Vietnam, during the spring of 1902. When faced with an outbreak of bubonic plague, the French colonialists offered a small fee for every rat's tail handed in. The tactic seemed successful at first – tails began to pour in. Hundreds each day in March and thousands in May, peaking on June 12th at a staggering 20,114.

But despite the growing tail collection, the rat population didn't appear to be declining. In fact, if anything, there were more rats – but they were tail-less. The bounty encouraged entrepreneurial spirits to feed rats, lop off their tails, and set them free.

From a safe distance this anecdote seems farcical. Yet poorly set targets still create problems today – everywhere from teaching-to-the-test, to risk-taking bankers. But most relevantly for our profession, in digital advertising.

Online measurement is delivering tails not rats

The key lesson from Hanoi is that setting a naive target encourages behaviour that superficially meets that goal rather than the underlying objective.

The targets set on most online activity measure short-term effects: immediate sales, visits, views. These short-term approaches are popular as they're easy to measure. However, ease and effectiveness are different. After all, we know that the bulk of advertising's effect is long-term.

Unfortunately, as it's hard to measure long-term impacts the tendency is to ignore them. Peter Field recently analysed the IPA Effectiveness Databank. This contains over 1,200 highly detailed entries into the IPA Effectiveness awards, which rigorously judge the return on investment that advertising delivers. He found that the proportion of entries with a short-term goal has risen from 7% in 2006 to 33% in 2014.

Marketers are like the drunk in the old joke:

> A policeman sees a drunk searching for something under a streetlight and asks what the drunk has lost. He says he has lost his keys and they both look under the streetlight together. After a few minutes the policeman asks if he is sure he lost them here, and the drunk replies, no. The policeman asks why he is searching here, and the drunk replies, "this is where the light is".

Marketers are optimising their campaigns to the easy-to-collect metrics, rather than the appropriate ones.

At first, optimising campaigns to short-term metrics seems successful: more budgets go to the best performers, while the worst are struck off the plan. But the success is illusory.

Les Binet and Peter Field proved in "The Long and Short of It", their earlier analysis of the IPA Effectiveness Databank, that what works best in the short term isn't ideal in the long term. Plans optimised to the short term deliver sales, not saleability. They convert those already interested in the brand to action, but they do nothing to grow the supply of people warm to the brand.

How to apply this effect

1. Introduce a balanced set of measurements

The simplest approach to improve digital measurement is to include multiple metrics on each plan. However, the metrics need to be balanced – some should monitor the short-term effect of the ads, others the long-term. This means complementing standard short-term metrics, such as cost per sale or cost per click, with long-term brand tracking.

There are competing approaches to brand tracking. The most popular is examining the difference in attitudes between those who recognise the ads and those who don't. The difference is then attributed to the impact of the advertising.

A simple approach, but misleading. It falls victim to the *Rosser Reeves fallacy*, named after the ad man who, back in 1961, first suggested the flawed approach. The method exaggerates the effect of ads: those familiar and warm to the brand are most likely to notice their ads.

Instead, digital brand tracking should measure the difference in attitudes between those in the target audience exposed to the ads and a control group, unexposed to the ads. This method has become simpler to undertake as many research companies have recruited panels of consumers willing to both supply their IP addresses and answer surveys. This allows the researchers to monitor who was actually exposed or not to the ads, rather than just those who remember being exposed.

The fetishisation of data is becoming commonplace.

Large digital campaigns only need to allocate about 1% of their media budget to fund this tracking. The learnings will quickly pay for themselves.

2. Allow room for discretion

A small but balanced mix of metrics will improve a brand's measurement approach. However, any set of metrics will be imperfect. Tracking data is reductive. It takes a complex, messy reality and converts it into easily manageable numbers. This process involves a trade-off: a loss of representativeness in return for simplicity.

Problems arise when the trade-off is forgotten and tracking data is treated with reverence, as if it was the definitive answer rather than mere evidence. The fetishisation of data is becoming commonplace. Marketing is in the grip, according to Rory Sutherland, of "a powerful left-brained administrative caste who attach importance only to things which can be expressed on a chart."

This obsession with easily quantified data crowds out the need for discretion and judgement.

Two examples illustrate the resulting issues. First is the experience of Terry Leahy who, when he was head of marketing at Tesco, analysed the performance of their gluten-free products. The sales data hinted it was an under-performing section – those that bought gluten-free goods only spent a few pounds on these items each shopping trip. A naive interpretation suggested de-listing them to free up valuable shelf space.

However, sceptical of the numbers, Leahy interviewed gluten-free shoppers and discovered that their choice of supermarket was determined by the availability of those products. They didn't want to make multiple shopping trips, so they visited whoever had the specialist goods. After all, every shop had milk and eggs but only some stocked gluten-free goods. Leahy used this insight to launch Tesco's hugely successful 'Free From' range long before the competition.

Another example, this time involving Manchester United manager, Sir Alex Ferguson, didn't have such a happy ending. Opta data showed that his star defender, Jaap Stam, was making fewer tackles each season. Ferguson promptly offloaded him in August 2001 to Lazio – keen to earn a high transfer fee before the decline became apparent to rival clubs.

However, Stam's career blossomed in Italy and Ferguson realised his error – the lower number of tackles was a sign of Stam's improvement, not decline. He was losing the ball less and intercepting more passes so that he needed to make fewer tackles. Ferguson says selling Stam was the biggest mistake of his managerial career. From then on he refused to be seduced by simplistic data.

These criticisms don't mean you should disregard tracking data. Expecting any methodology to be perfect is to burden it with unreasonable expectations. Instead, you need to be aware that it merely provides evidence to which you need to apply your discretion and judgement.

If you've been guilty of putting too much emphasis on short-term tracking data don't hide the fact. Let your colleagues know about your mistake. It might be counter-intuitive but this admission of weakness will make you more appealing. At least, that's the finding of Elliot Aronson, who coined the term "pratfall effect". It's to Aronson's work that we turn now.

BIAS 18

The Pratfall Effect

*How flaws make a brand
more appealing*

> Your main task this afternoon is to interview the last two candidates for the position of manager on your team. At the close of the second interview you realise both candidates have the same relevant experience, strong academic results and practical ideas to implement once they start. You're wondering how you'll ever choose between them. As the final candidate gets up to leave, he catches his foot awkwardly on the table leg, upending the dregs of his coffee over the new floor. He leaves ashen-faced.

W**HO DO YOU** think you'll end up picking? If the pratfall effect is correct, it'll be the clumsy candidate.

The bias was discovered in 1966 by Harvard University psychologist Elliot Aronson. Along with his colleagues, Ben Willerman and Joanne Floyd, he recorded an actor answering a series of quiz questions. In one strand of the experiment, the actor – armed with the right responses – answers 92% of the questions correctly. After the quiz, the actor then pretends to spill a cup of coffee over himself (a small blunder, or pratfall).

The recording was played to a large sample of students, who were then asked how likeable the contestant was. However, Aronson split the students into cells and played them different versions: one with the spillage included and one without. The students found the clumsy contestant more likeable. In Aronson's words:

> The pratfall made the contestant more appealing as it increases his approachability and makes him seem less austere, more human.

Does the bias work on products sixty years later?

It's not just clumsiness that increases appeal. Jenny Riddell and I investigated whether product flaws could boost appeal. We replicated an unpublished study by consumer psychologist Adam Ferrier by asking 626 nationally representative people which of two cookies they preferred. The biscuits were identical apart from one small difference: one had a rough edge; the other a perfectly smooth one.

The cookie with the rough edge was the overwhelming favourite: 66% preferred it. The small imperfection didn't detract from its appeal, but boosted it.

How to apply this effect

1. Flaunt your flaws

The best application is to admit that your brand has a flaw.

Foolhardy?

Not if you consider how many of the leading ad campaigns have done so.

One of the earliest examples was the long-running American VW ad campaign by Doyle Dane Bernbach, which from 1959, gloried in the flaws of the Beetle. The looks of the car were gently mocked with one print ad featuring a photo of the lunar module and the headline, "It's ugly but it gets you there". Another referenced the size of the car with the line "Think Small". And my favourite drew attention to the slow speed in the body copy: "A VW won't go over 72 mph. (Even though the speedometer shows a wildly optimistic top speed of 90.)"

The trade magazine *Ad Age* ranked it the best ad of the 20th century. More importantly, it shifted a lot of cars. In 1963 VW sold 277,008 vehicles in the US – more than any other imported brand had ever sold.

Bill Bernbach's agency repeated the honest approach with Avis. The tagline, written by Paula Green, emphasised the car rental's relative unpopularity compared to Hertz: "When you're only number two you try harder. Or else." Within a year of the campaign launching, Avis made a profit of $1.2m – the first time they had broken even in a decade. The approach was so successful it ran for more than 50 years.

Then there's Lowe's campaign for Stella Artois, beginning in 1981, which revelled in its high price under the headline, "Reassuringly Expensive". The award-winning campaign transformed Stella's fortunes and ran for 26 years.

Guinness and AMV publicised the slowness of the pour with "Good things come to those who wait". The National Dairy Council alluded to the high calorific content of cream cakes with "Naughty, but Nice". (Incidentally, that strapline was coined by Salman Rushdie while working at Ogilvy & Mather.)

Admitting weakness is a tangible demonstration of honesty and, therefore, makes other claims more believable. Further to that, the best straplines harness the trade-off effect. We know from bitter experience that we don't get anything for free in life. By admitting a weakness, a brand credibly establishes a related positive attribute.

Guinness may take longer to pour but boy, it's worth it. Avis might not have the most sales but it's desperate to keep you happy.

Everyone assumes that brands are fallible, so if a brand is open about its failings, it can persuade consumers that its weaknesses lie in inconsequential areas. This theory partly explains the success of budget airlines. At launch they openly admitted that the trade-off for cheap prices was compromised service: no seat reservations and a pitiful luggage allowance. If they hadn't admitted as much, consumers may have assumed the cost-cutting had come at the expense of safety.

2. Make sure this tactic suits your brand

A twist in Aronson's experiment suggests caution. He repeated the set-up but this time the actor feigned incompetence and answered only 30% of the questions correctly. Once again students rated his appeal. In this scenario the clumsy spillage made him less appealing. The pratfall effect has a multiplicative effect rather than a purely positive one. It makes strong brands stronger, but weak brands weaker.

> The pratfall effect works particularly well when the competitors are braggards.

The pratfall effect works particularly well when the competitors are braggards. And nowhere is hyperbole more prevalent than among estate agents. Roy Brooks carved out a profitable niche in the 1960s by selling houses in a brutally honest manner. Here's a typical ad:

> Wanted: Someone with taste, means and a stomach strong enough to buy this erstwhile house of ill-repute in Pimlico. It is untouched by the 20th century as far as conveniences for even the basic human decencies are concerned. Although it reeks of damp or worse, the plaster is coming off the walls and daylight peeps through a hole in the roof, it is still habitable judging by the bed of rags, fag ends and empty bottles in one corner. Plenty of scope for the socially aspiring to express their decorative taste and get their abode in The Glossy, and nothing to stop them putting Westminster on their notepaper.

Comprises 10 rather unpleasant rooms with slimy back yard,
4,650 Freehold. Tarted up, these houses make 15,000.

In another ad he honestly appraised the rickety stairs in a house for
sale:

A lightly-built member of our staff negotiated the basement
stair, but our Mr Halstead went crashing through.

Nor were buyers spared:

WE HAVE A RATHER REPULSIVE OLD MAN who
with his child-wife, are looking for an elegant town res. pref
Belgravia…Price not important but must be realistic as he has,
at least, his head screwed on the right way…

Brooks' bravado paid off. His unique style earned untold levels of
publicity: readers of the Sunday papers made a habit of seeking out
his ads and he regularly appeared on TV chat shows. If you work in a
category typified by overly positive descriptions, such as luxuries, cars
or cosmetics, then this approach might be suitable.

It's also worth considering the gender of your target audience.
Kay Deaux, Professor of Psychology at New York City University,
conducted an experiment in 1972 that showed that men are more
swayed by the pratfall effect than women. If your brand targets men
then admitting weaknesses should be an approach you seriously
consider.

3. More than just ads

Finally, it's not just a matter of tweaking the copy in your ads. It should
affect how you deal with unflattering customer reviews. Many brands
hide their negative reviews. However, a 2015 study, by Northwestern
University's Spiegel Research Centre, analysed 111,460 product reviews
across 22 categories and linked ratings to probability of purchasing. It
found that likelihood of purchase didn't peak with perfect scores but
at 4.2-4.5 out of 5. There was only minor variation between categories
– hair care reviews, for example, peaked in effectiveness at 4.2, while
4.5 was ideal for light bulbs.

Perfect ratings had less impact because they were seen as too good to be true. According to the authors:

> Counter-intuitive as it may seem, but negative reviews may have a positive impact because they help establish trust and authenticity. Consumers understand that a product can't be all things to all people.

My favourite such example comes from Iain Banks's 1984 debut novel, *The Wasp Factory*. Banks was thirty when he finally persuaded a publisher to release one of his works. The delay was not for want of trying. Over the previous 14 years he had written four novels, all of which had been rejected by publishers.

Despite struggling for so long to gain recognition, Banks broke with tradition and insisted that the novel included both positive and negative reviews within the blurb. Some of the reviews were caustic, such as the following from the *Sunday Express*:

> A silly, gloatingly sadistic and grisly yarn of a family of Scots lunatics, one of whom tortures small creatures – a bit better written than most horror hokum but really just the literary equivalent of a video nasty.

The *Times* was even more damning:

> As a piece of writing, The Wasp Factory soars to the level of mediocrity. Maybe the crassly explicit language, the obscenity of the plot were thought to strike an agreeably avant-garde note. Perhaps it's all a joke meant to fool literary London into respect for rubbish.

Banks's chutzpah paid off. His distinctive approach got him noticed and the sheer outrage of many critics meant its positioning as a powerfully moving book had credibility. The publicity helped create a bestseller, while positioning him as an independent thinker.

If it's a successful approach, why is it rare?

I have listed half a dozen examples of the pratfall effect and there are a handful of others. But they stretch over a period of nearly 60 years, making them a minuscule proportion of the tens of thousands of ads that have run over that time.

Why?

The rarity is explained by the principal-agent problem, a theory first suggested by Stephen Ross, Professor of Finance at the MIT Sloan School of Management. He suggested that there is a divergence between the interest of the principal in a company, the shareholders, and the agent, the staff.

> The best chance of growing your brand is to flaunt your flaws.

What is in the interest of the brand, the principal, is not in the interest of the marketing manager, the agent. If the campaign flops it might be the end of the brand manager's career. Imagine explaining to your CEO as sales dive that the key message of your campaign was that the brand was expensive. Even referencing Aronson's research won't save you.

For those prepared to embrace a modicum of career risk then the best chance of growing your brand is to flaunt your flaws. The principal-agent problem ensures it will always be a distinctive approach. For those interested in safe career progression then you may want to consider another route, such as avoiding the winner's curse. Luckily for you that's what the next chapter is about.

BIAS 19

Winner's Curse

---

*Why digital media buying
is blighted by it*

> You're up to date on your emails, so you decide to take a moment to check eBay – you're bidding for a *Game of Thrones* box-set and the auction is due to end this afternoon.
>
> Oh dear. You've been outbid. You up your offer by a fiver. No luck, you're still not winning.
>
> Bastard.
>
> Another fiver. Then another. Until finally, you're ahead.

Y OUR SATISFACTION AT edging ahead in the auction might be unwarranted. Economists believe that the winner of an auction typically pays over the odds, as a result of something they call the *winner's curse*.

The phrase dates back to the 1950s when a spate of oil companies significantly overpaid at an auction for Alaskan drilling rights. Some paid so far over the odds that they went bust. Economists, such as Richard Thaler, investigated the problem and came up with an elegant explanation.

Thaler, Professor of Behavioural Science and Economics at the University of Chicago, believes that during an auction each bidder makes a private valuation of the goods and then bids up to that amount.

Due to a phenomenon known as the wisdom of the crowds, the average of all those valuations is reasonably accurate. After all, averaging out the valuations will balance out the errors that each bidder makes. But of course, if the average valuation is accurate, then the winning bid – the most optimistic in its valuation – must be inflated.

Why does the winner's curse matter to you?

The cost of media is the single biggest advertising expenditure for most brands. In 2015 £20bn was spent on advertising media in the UK, according to the WARC/AA report.

The manner in which space is bought has changed radically in the last ten years. It has morphed from a system where advertisers negotiated a fixed cost per thousand from media owners, to one where buyers compete in an auction. In this new approach, advertisers bid in real-time for individual digital impressions.

Not all media is bought via auctions but it is an increasingly important approach. All of search and most of programmatic display advertising is bought via an auction. According to the Internet Advertising Bureau these two areas accounted for £8.75bn of spend in 2016. As programmatic spreads to other media, such as radio, mobile and, eventually, TV, that number will grow even further.

How to apply this effect

1. Find unique ways of identifying your target audience

Auctions are here to stay. Brands can't ignore them. Instead they need to adapt their bidding tactics by creating a contrarian set of metrics to identify their audience.

Most brands target their media based on age and income, such as whether they are 18–34s or ABC1s. As this is the standard approach, any brand using it will be involved in highly competitive auctions. And the more participants in an auction, the more accurate the average bid and the harder it is to escape the winner's curse.

The formulaic targeting of most brands means there are opportunities for canny brands. One under-exploited opportunity is to target people by the browser they use.

Can browser usage really identify the right customers?

Dr Michael Housman, Chief Analytics Officer at Cornerstone OnDemand, pioneered the idea that people's characteristics could be identified by their browser.

He analysed data from 50,000 people who his recruitment software company had helped find jobs and discovered that browser choice accurately predicted their performance. People who opted for a non-default browser, like Chrome or Firefox, lasted 15% longer in their jobs than those with a default browser, like Internet Explorer.

Housman attributed the difference to the fact that choosing Chrome or Firefox was an active decision – those workers were taking the effort to find a better browsing solution than the one pre-installed on their PC. That identified them as someone who wasn't content with the default.

What's the marketing application?

Clare Linford and I wondered if Housman's findings could also be useful for marketers. Perhaps people who avoid the mainstream, default browser choice, might do the same in other product categories?

We tested this hypothesis by questioning 224 lager drinkers about their brand of choice. When we split the results by their favoured browser the results were clear-cut. Only a third of lager drinkers who used Internet Explorer preferred a beer from outside the mainstream, top five lagers. However, 56% of those who didn't use a default browser preferred a non-mainstream lager.

Default browser users preferred mainstream choices, non-default browser users liked challenger brands. Just as browser choice gave Housman a clue about job performance, it can identify brand preference for marketers.

Since ads can be targeted by browser type you can easily put this information to profitable use: mainstream brands should target default browsers, such as Internet Explorer, and less orthodox choices should target non-default browsers, like Google Chrome.

Crucially, it's a signal that is rarely used by brands so it helps avoid the winner's curse.

When it comes to identifying target audiences, brands need to remember the words of legendary creative director, John Hegarty:

When the world zigs, zag.

2. Identify the moment when a target audience becomes valuable

Advertisers target ABC1s because they have a high disposable income. However, people's spending patterns are not flat. There are regular and predictable moments when their spending spikes. One such moment is payday.

Jenny Riddell and I surveyed 200 consumers about their monthly spending patterns. The biggest change was an uplift in spend the week after being paid. A third of adults spent a little or a lot more.

When we split the data by the respondent's age we discovered that the uplift was most pronounced amongst 18–34s, with nearly half (47%) spending more. This was probably due to that group having lower incomes, meaning they were more likely to have run out of cash by the end of the month.

Crucially, payday is a predictable moment. 64% of our sample claimed to be paid at the end of the month.

Our findings should be treated with caution as they were based on claimed data. However, they are supported by an experiment by Matthew Shapiro, Professor of Economics at the University of Michigan, which didn't rely on claims.

He used data from *Check*, a smartphone app that tracks account balances, to monitor the spending patterns of 23,000 people across 300 days. This showed that, on average, payday spend spikes by 70%. Even when bills are stripped out the rise amounted to more than 40% and lasted for roughly four days. Shapiro, worried that some of that uplift might be from bills he'd inadvertently missed, analysed specific categories, like fast food and coffee, where

> On average, payday spend spikes by 70%.

there was an uplift of 20% for three or four days after payday. Again, the uplifts were not uniform: low-income groups were particularly prone to splurging after payday.

Payday is not the only moment when customers spend more. Any time consumers receive a windfall, like birthdays or bonuses, they will increase their spending. Three Ohio University psychologists, Hal Arkes, Cynthia Joyner and Mark Prezzo, ran an experiment in 1994 exploring this phenomenon. When they recruited students for the experiment half were told a week before that they would be paid $3, while the rest expected to be given course credits. However, when the participants arrived at the experiment they were all given the same $3-dollar incentive.

The participants were given the chance to gamble with their cash on a simple dice game. Those who had been given cash in the windfall condition gambled on average $2.16 while those who had been fully expecting the money only frittered away $1.

> Unearned money was more likely to be spent on clothes, alcohol, tobacco and gifts.

The finding that windfalls are more likely to be splurged than standard income, has been repeated in a broad range of settings. Luc Christiaensen, an economist at the World Bank, found similar findings in Tanzania and China. Unearned money was more likely to be spent on clothes, alcohol, tobacco and gifts whereas earned money tended to go on staple foods and education.

This has repercussions for targeting. As it's expensive to target ABC1s, an alternative is to reach more downmarket groups at the predictable moments when they are spending at the same rate as ABC1s.

3. Convert better

One tactic to avoid the winner's curse is to ensure that you're squeezing more value out of the impressions you buy than your competition. That way, even if one of your competitors bids more than the impression is worth to them, they can still be profitable for you.

There are two basic tactics:

1. Ensure your impressions are more likely to be noticed and acted upon than your competition. Here it might be worth looking at Bias 4 and the power of distinctiveness.

2. Ensure that once consumers have reached your site you convert them as effectively as possible.

4. Bid shaving

The final option is the simplest of all. If there's a tendency to over-pay, then recognise this and shave a little bit off your bids. If you estimate that a thousand impressions are worth £5 then reduce that bid by, say, 10%, to £4.50.

In the case of the winner's curse, groups create problems. It's hard to outsmart the collective mind of the market. However, groups aren't always troublesome. When it comes to targeting ads it can be more effective to reach people when they're in groups. If you turn to the next page I'll show you the evidence.

BIAS 20

The Power of the Group

*Why targeting groups
boosts ad effectiveness*

> 4.03 pm...
>
> You check your watch again... 4.07pm...
>
> The afternoon is dragging on. After checking your emails, and finishing your timesheets you call it quits for the day.
>
> You decide to watch some clips of Alan Partridge on YouTube. The first show you find is the one where Alan ineptly interviews an increasingly irate farmer. The interview ends with him accusing the farmer of making pigs smoke and feeding burgers to swans. You try and stifle a laugh and it comes out like a snort.

PART OF THE reason you found the clips funny was the use of canned laughter. TV producers have long realised that if you hear other people laughing the same material will seem funnier. In fact, the insight stretches back further than the history of TV or radio.

Instances of theatre impresarios paying people to sit in the audience and show their appreciation stretch all the way back to the 16th century.

These stooges became such an accepted occurrence that by the 19th century theatre managers could hire not just specialists in the art of laughing, but also *claquers*, (who focused on clapping), *pleureurs* (who could cry on demand) and even *bisseurs* (who called out "encore").

Theatre impresarios paid handsomely for these services as they realised that a great performance didn't just come from the stage.

As the ballet critic, Vadim Gayevsky, said:

> The audience does not trust itself, it trusts someone else. If they hear someone applauding very aggressively and intensively, they think that something extraordinary is going on.

How the group dynamic affects ads

The contagious effect of humour explains the results of a 1991 experiment conducted by University of Houston psychologists, Yong Zhang and George Zinkan.

They recruited 216 students to watch 30 minutes of music videos interspersed with soft drink commercials in groups of one, three and six. In order for the test to be as realistic as possible, the participants were told they were going to be questioned on their music preferences.

Their key finding was that ads tended to be rated as least funny when they were watched alone. In contrast, ads watched in groups of three and six were reported to be 21% and 10%, funnier than those watched alone.

The impact of groups might be due to social proof – this is the idea that people are influenced by others' behaviour. If one person laughs, it encourages others to find the content funny.

What can brands learn from the social nature of humour?

The key point is that the funniness of an ad is not solely a creative issue but also one of media placement. You can boost the perception of funniness of an ad by showing it to groups, rather than lone viewers.

The group affects more than just laughter

The impact of group size goes beyond funny ads. In 2014 Garriy Shteynberg, Assistant Professor of Social Psychology at the University of Tennessee, and his team recruited 121 students and showed them 30 images on a TV. The participants, who watched on their own or in pairs, had to rate their feelings as they saw each picture.

When the academics controlled for gender and prior mood they found that viewers in a group experienced more extreme reactions: happy images made them happier and sad images made them sadder. They found similar effects when they showed other participants scary ads and sad or happy videos.

Shteynberg explains this from an evolutionary angle. For most of our history humans have been dependent on groups for their survival. If the rest of the group gave their attention to an event it was worth copying.

How to apply this effect

Prioritise group viewing moments

The experiments I have mentioned show that the effect of funny or emotional ads becomes magnified if they are viewed in groups.

If you have TV copy you can increase the probability that it is seen by groups by a judicious selection of genres and programmes. For example, films, documentaries and news are roughly twice as likely as TV as a whole to be watched in groups, according to Infosys data.

From a channel planning perspective, running humorous or emotional copy in cinema is another opportunity as it means the ad will be consumed in much larger groups. According to the industry measurement survey, FAME, when adults visit the cinema their average group size is 2.7.

In 2009 Millward Brown publicised research that quantified the impact. In their experiment an unnamed brand ran the same piece of copy in two regions. One region just aired TV while the other just had cinema.

Those who saw the cinema ad enjoyed it considerably more than the TV ad – with 61% saying they "enjoyed the humour" compared to 52% of the TV viewers. Furthermore, the cinema ad outperformed the same copy by 21% to 15% on the other metric monitored, "it's the sort of ad that sticks in your mind".

Applying these approaches won't transform a mediocre ad into a great one but it might just give it an edge over copy bought in a more generic manner. If transformation is what you're after then the next chapter might be of interest. It's all about the power of price...

BIAS 21

Veblen Goods

How a high price can boost demand

As it's a colleague's birthday one of your team has organised a surprise: a caterpillar cake and a few glasses of bubbly. The champagne hits the spot perfectly – cold, refreshing with a subtly sweet aftertaste. You drain your glass and head to the kitchen for a little more.

There are a couple of half-drunk bottles of sparkling wine on the work surface. It wasn't champagne after all, and according to the price tag, it was £4.99 from the off licence.

You refill your glass and have a sip – maybe, on second thoughts, the sweetness is just a little cloying.

Your enjoyment of the wine is being influenced by the price. Experience has taught you that expensive products tend to be higher quality. It's such an ingrained belief that it becomes self-fulfilling.

THE POWER OF price in steering perceptions has been studied by Dan Ariely, Professor of Psychology and Behavioural Economics at Duke University. In 2008 he recruited 82 participants from

Craigslist who were willing to receive two small electric shocks in the name of science: one before taking a painkiller and one after. Half the participants were told the painkiller cost $2.50 a dose and half that it was only 10c. In fact, they all received placebos.

Of those taking the cheaper pill only 61% reported less pain compared to 85% among those taking the more expensive version. The high price of the pill led to an assumption that it would be more effective and this assumption shaped the actual perception.

The sweet smell of expensive perfume

Intrigued by these results, Rebecca Strong and I organised an experiment among our colleagues to test the commercial application. We set up a stall in reception with a wide range of perfumes, each labelled with its price. As staff arrived they sampled the perfumes and rated their likelihood to purchase.

Half way through the test we switched the labels on the test perfume and doubled its price, from £40 to £80. This small change had a big effect. Staff were more than twice as likely to rate the perfume highly at the higher price. At the lower price only 33% rated the perfume seven or higher on a scale of ten. In contrast, this figure rose to 78% at the higher price. Yet again, price signalled quality, independent of any change in the underlying product.

How to apply this effect

1. A portfolio approach

Many brands have a portfolio of products ranging in quality and price. Think of Tesco who have a Value, Standard and Finest offering. Or Audi, whose product range straddles entry-level cars to high-end models.

The standard advertising budget setting approach is to allocate funds according to the sales volumes of each line. However, these experiments suggest an alternative for any brand struggling with quality perceptions. As price conveys quality, canny brands should invest disproportionately behind their higher end goods. This conveys an aura of quality that radiates across the entire portfolio.

This is Audi's strategy. Its lower cost models rarely appear on TV. Instead this medium is reserved for the most appealing, and invariably expensive, models. Even the low selling R8, their six-figure sports car, has featured on TV.

A more extreme approach is to launch a high-end variant. This was McDonald's thinking when in 2015 they launched the Signature burger, priced at £4.69. The burger designed by chefs from Michelin starred restaurants, cooked to order and served in a brioche bun, acts as a convincing signal of quality.

It's crucial that this approach is measured accurately. Don't judge success by sales of the higher-end variant but on how overall perceptions of the brand have changed.

2. Discounters beware

If high prices boost perceptions, then what does a low price do? Baba Shiv, Professor of Marketing at Stanford, attempted to find out.

Shiv recruited students to answer maths puzzles and paid them a small sum for every correct answer. Before the students were tested they were allowed to buy a caffeinated energy drink which would supposedly focus their mind. Half of the students were sold the drink at full price, while half bought it at a discount. Those who bought the reduced price energy drinks answered 30% fewer questions correctly. Low prices damage our expectation of a product just as much as high prices boost them.

This should seriously worry the many brands who boost market share by dropping their price. What works in the short term will damage their desirability in the long term.

More than 40% of all groceries sold in the UK are sold on promotion.

Sir Martin Sorrell, CEO of WPP, coined an interesting dietary analogy. Promotions are like "bad cholesterol": they boost sales but at a cost to brand health. In contrast, advertising is akin to "good cholesterol": it delivers sales while maintaining profitability and brand equity.

Just as it's fine to have a little bad cholesterol in your diet, so it's fine to indulge in the occasional promotion. However, brands are not dabbling with the odd promotion, they are dangerously addicted. Recent figures from *Which?* reveal that more than 40% of all groceries sold in the UK are sold on promotion.

For their long-term health, brands need to shun promotions over prolonged periods.

3. Consider your research sample

One criticism of behavioural science is that the research samples are unrepresentative. They often use the easiest audience to recruit – students – rather than the most representative.

It's a fair critique. The perfume experiment was one of the first I ever undertook, and using staff limited its value. If I repeated it I'd recruit members of the public. It would be simple – set up a stall on the high street and then stop people with the promise of an incentive. The most effective reward I've found is a £1 lottery scratch card. It's cheap and tends to be more effective than cash.

It's also worth noting that size alone does not make a data set robust: it needs to be representative, a point that has been forgotten in the rush to embrace Big Data. Tim Harford, the FT columnist, gives the example of Boston's *Street Bump* app that uses a smartphone's accelerometer to record when a car hits a pothole. The council then used that data to direct where their repair trucks went. A brilliant advance on the previous technique of sending workmen out to prowl the roads looking for potholes.

Just one problem...

In the words of Harford:

> What Street Bump really produces, left to its own devices, is a map of potholes that systematically favours young, affluent areas where more people own smartphones. Street Bump offers us "N = All" in the sense that every bump from every enabled phone can be recorded. That is not the same thing as recording every pothole.

Another danger is that in the rush for accuracy there's a danger that your test design becomes too complex. This means they become expensive and that limits the number you undertake. That is worse than a rough and ready test. The point of these tests isn't to answer the question with 100% certainty; it's to give you enough evidence to run a larger-scale test with your advertising message.

The worries about behavioural science extend beyond representative samples. Critics, like Brian Nosek, are concerned that some experiments have failed to be replicated. Luckily, we'll be discussing replicability in the next chapter.

BIAS 22

The Replicability Crisis

How should marketers react?

> Your first sip of coffee causes you to wince. For the last fortnight, each hot drink has been accompanied by a twinge in your back tooth.
>
> You decide to ring your dentist to arrange an appointment before it deteriorates any further.
>
> The receptionist answers within a few rings and, after expressing her concern, she checks the dentist's availability. "I'm afraid", she says, "Thursday at 10am is the only time that you can be seen by Dennis."
>
> You book the slot and, as you put the phone down, smile at the similarity of his name and profession.

THE IDEA THAT people are attracted to careers linked to their names is called *nominative determinism*. Examples include: Mark de Man, a Belgian footballer; Sara Blizzard, a BBC weather reporter, and Ann Webb, author of the book, *Proper Care of Tarantulas*. My favourite though, comes from 1923 when the neurology journal, *Brain*, was looking for a new chief to succeed Sir Henry Head. His replacement was the even more aptly named, Lord Brain.

The concept has a long history of famous supporters. In 1952 the psychoanalyst, Carl Jung, said that there was a "sometimes quite grotesque coincidence between a man's name and his peculiarities". He noted that Sigmund Freud, who was famous for coming up with the pleasure principle, had a surname that was translated as "joy".

The theory isn't just supported by anecdotes. There's experimental evidence too. In 2002, three psychologists, Brett Pelham, Matthew Mirenberg and John Jones, at the State University of New York at Buffalo, published a paper entitled, "Why Susie sells seashells by the seashore". Their analysis of US census data found 88% more dentists called Dennis than Walter, even though the names are just as common.

The academics speculated that implicit egotism was the cause; people feel warm towards their names and this attracts them to activities that sound similar. It's a plausible explanation.

But there's a problem. It's not true.

Anna sells seashells by the sea shore, as well as Susie

As convincing as the anecdotes, explanations and evidence sound, they're not backed by rigorous evidence. The theory was demolished in 2011 by Uri Simonsohn of the Wharton School. He pointed out that Dennis was the more common name among most professions. The simple explanation was that Walter might have the same total popularity but it was a name favoured overwhelmingly by older generations. People called Dennis were simply more likely to be of working age.

Nominative determinism is not the only theory to be debunked. Brian Nosek, Professor of Psychology at the University of Virginia, has tried to cleanse the discipline of rogue findings. He recruited 270 scientists to replicate 98 published psychology experiments. A worryingly low percentage produced the same results as the original.

Depending on the statistical measure used, only 36% to 47% of studies were successfully replicated.

But why such a low rate?

Suggestions have ranged from outright fraud to p-hacking. That's the term for blindly testing dozens of variables in the hope that, by sheer fluke, some show statistically significant results.

Nosek's work should make us cautious and not place too much weight on results backed by only a single experiment.

How to apply this effect

1. Be sceptical, not cynical

Nosek's series of experiments has generated much publicity. Some critics of psychology have suggested the discipline should be ignored. Byron Sharp, Professor of Marketing Science at the University of South Australia, derides psychological findings as the "show ponies" or "delicate flowers" of the research world.

But is he right to dismiss the discipline?

Dan Gilbert, Professor of Psychology at Harvard University, suggests caution. He has critiqued a number of elements of Nosek's methodology. He has highlighted that some of the new studies weren't faithful copies of the originals. This is a concern because context is one of the core principles of social psychology and therefore must be kept constant for true replication to be tested. Others have added that the type of scientists drawn to participate in this project might be biased and want to debunk cases.

However, Gilbert's most damning criticism is that the replication was attempted just once. Nosek's previous work, called the Many Labs Replication Project, tried multiple replications with 36 labs aiming to replicate 13 studies. When the results were taken as an entirety the project validated 10 out of the 13 studies, but if just one lab's findings had been analysed it would have suggested that many of the studies failed to replicate.

It's true that some studies are flawed, that some might even be bogus, but it's an overreaction to dismiss the whole field. If you reject psychology in its entirety, then why not dismiss other academic disciplines?

Don't take a single study as definitive proof.

Daniele Fanelli, Senior Research Scientist at Stanford University, suggested in *Nature* that reproducibility could be more of an issue in drug discovery and cancer biology. Furthermore, in 2016 Colin Camerer, Professor of Behavioral Finance and Economics at Caltech, published a study which found that seven out of 18 economics studies failed to replicate (dropping to four if a different statistical measure was used). This is clearly an issue that affects disciplines beyond psychology.

Rejecting psychological, or economic, findings as a whole is impractical. However, Nosek's work suggests that you should be cautious. Don't take a single study as definitive proof. If you believe you have found a relevant bias, test it on a small scale before investing too much.

Proceed with caution, but do not fall into the trap of cynicism.

2. Marketers should be concerned with profit, not certainty

The standard measure that academics use to judge whether findings are deemed worthy of publication is whether they are significant at 95%. This means that there is only a 1 in 20 chance that the results are random. It was this threshold that Nosek applied in his replication study.

But is 95% the right benchmark?

The choice of this particular figure is arbitrary. William Sealy Gossett, one of the founders of statistical significance (the Student's t-distribution was created by him) argued that the degree of certainty required should reflect the problem you face.

> Many marketing decisions do not require 95% certainty.

Imagine you're about to cross the road. A 95% certainty that you'll avoid a car is a dangerously low threshold for action. However, if you're offered a bet at evens odds you shouldn't insist on anything like the same level of certainty. If you only accepted bets when you were that sure, you would miss out on many chances to win. There are costs to not acting, as well as acting.

Gossett's sensitivity to context was probably related to his commercial, rather than academic, background. Gosset worked at Guinness and was interested in using statistics to pick the best yielding varieties of barley. His aim was to maximise profits, not deliver absolute certainty.

Many marketing decisions do not require 95% certainty. Rory Sutherland says:

> I occasionally ask academics whether they have any interesting failed experiments we can use. You see if just 20% of people do something anomalous 10% of the time, that's useless in academic papers but relevant to business.

> Voraciously hunt for new experiments being conducted by psychologists.

If the potential upside is large and the downside is minimal, then insisting on 95% certainty is misguided. This risk profile exists in many marketing situations.

Suppose you have just read a paper that suggests people are more likely to notice ads if they're in a good mood. Your next step should be to instigate a small test. If this new targeting approach is no better than your historic methods, then you don't run it again. Nothing much has been lost. However, if it outperforms your control then you can repeat it again and again, each time on a bigger scale. The odds are stacked in your favour: failures happen once, successes live on.

This should inspire you to voraciously hunt for new experiments being conducted by psychologists. Each time one looks promising run a small-scale test. When you're measuring the impact of a bias make sure that you split out the variable effect on each audience. Recent work, which will be covered in the next few pages, has shown that biases effect different people in a variety of ways...

BIAS 23

Variability

How biases affect segments in different ways

You specifically suggested this pub as it has a good range of ales. As you squeeze your way to the bar, you're unsure of what to buy, so you inspect the pumps. You normally choose a dark beer but a glass on top of the pump shows that the Half Moon porter has sold out.

You look at the IPAs instead. The Brockwell IPA has a sign saying it's this week's most popular beer. It looks drinkable, but the Tall Trees Session IPA isn't as strong, which, considering how much you have already knocked back, is appealing.

The barman is approaching so you make a snap decision. "A pint of Tall Trees, please," you hear yourself say, "and two bags of salt and vinegar crisps."

IN BIAS 2 I outlined the effectiveness of social proof. Social proof messages are ones that indicate to consumers which choice is the most popular.

Robert Cialdini, Professor of Psychology at Arizona State University, showed with his experiment into towel re-use that, regardless of customer claims, social proof messages can dramatically alter behaviour. The power of social proof has been demonstrated in a wide variety of scenarios, from smoking to food choices, and from music downloads to tax collection. Most pertinent to this situation, Richard Clay and I demonstrated that social proof influences beer choice.

So why didn't it work on you tonight?

Nudges aren't magic. They don't transform the behaviour of every person, every time. The clue is in the name: they're nudges, not shoves. They make it more likely that, in general, people will behave in a particular way.

But why are some people affected and not others?

Recent work has explored this further.

When is social proof most effective?

One of the most famous experiments from the Behavioural Insight Team, the unit established to spread behavioural best practice through UK governmental departments, showed that social proof encouraged timelier tax payments. As we saw earlier in the book, a message saying, "Most people pay their tax on time" led to a 15% increase in the number who paid before the deadline.

What is less well known is that it affected people in different ways. The variance was so extreme that in some groups, the social proof message backfired completely. For example, compared to the control, social proof messaging resulted in 25% *lower* collections among the top 5% of debtors. The situation was even more extreme among the top 1%, who owed upwards of £30,000. Their repayment levels dropped by a massive 35% when social proof messaging was used.

David Halpern, CEO of the Behavioural Insight Team, hypothesised that those running large businesses with sizeable tax bills viewed themselves as unique, which rendered social proof counter-productive: they believe that the behaviour of others is irrelevant to them.

Given this fascinating finding, the Behavioural Insight Team decided to explore further. In 2015 they ran a test among 98,784 debtors to understand which message would work best among the biggest debtors.

The most effective message focused on the repercussions of unpaid tax: it emphasised that we all lose out on public services, such as the NHS, when tax isn't paid on time. This loss framing boosted payment rates by 8% among the top 5% of debtors, and an enormous 43% among the highest 1% of debtors.

So, clearly, a one size fits all approach is not ideal. The most effective solution, in the case of tax collection, was to run a broad social proof message, complemented by a loss message to the highest taxpayers.

How to apply this effect

1. Don't rest on your laurels

It's tempting to introduce nudges, see improved results and then consider your work complete. However, the experience of the Behavioural Insight Team shows that you can eke out improvements by segmenting your approach. This necessitates running tests with large sample sizes so that you can split them by demographic, attitudinal and behavioural groups. Although this will make the research more expensive, it can lead to significant improvements.

When I spoke to Owain Service, Managing Director of the Behavioural Insight Team, he advised running simple experiments first. Once you have shown nudging is valuable to your business then progress to larger, more complex segmentations.

Once you have segmented your data and understood the relative impact of the bias you're testing – such as social proof – you must refine your strategy. If there are groups who react negatively to a bias, test an alternative.

2. Match the bias to the task

A bias that works in one situation might backfire in another. That makes matching the bias to the task essential. To select the most appropriate nudge, you need to understand what purpose it is playing.

Take scarcity and social proof. Social proof is based on a general belief that if lots of people are doing it, it must be good. This can be explained from an evolutionary perspective as it would have been an effective self-protection strategy: when threatened, there is safety in numbers.

> A bias that works in one situation might backfire in another.

In contrast, scarcity explains why limited editions are appealing: consumers think if it's rare it must be worth having. From an evolutionary perspective this also makes sense, but this time in the realm of mating. A strategy that successfully attracts mates is to stand out from the crowd: whether that's a peacock displaying its plumage or conspicuous consumption.

In other words, don't apply biases randomly – employ scarcity at romantic moments and social proof at fearful ones.

Research from Vladas Griskevicus, Professor of Marketing and Psychology at the University of Minnesota, supports this observation.

He and his team recruited 154 students to watch either scary or romantic video clips. To scare participants, they showed a seven-minute clip of the horror movie, *The Shining;* to put the others in a romantic mood, they screened *Before Sunset*.

Dubious?

When I first read that part of the experiment I was sceptical. Can a video clip really elicit a specified mood? However, the researchers double-checked. They recruited an additional 96 students and showed the videos in question. Afterwards the viewers rated their mood. The results showed that the stimulus had the intended effect.

Once in the correct mindset, the original participants were shown ads for either a museum or a café. Each ad had two versions: a social proof version and a scarcity one. So, for example, the museum was either described as being a unique experience or a popular one. After glancing at the ads for 15 seconds they rated the appeal of the ads on a nine-point scale.

The scared students rated the social proof message most appealing: it outperformed the scarcity message by 31%. In contrast, the romantically aroused audience preferred the scarcity message; it outperformed the social proof one by 30%.

And the title of the paper? Since some of the ads were set in Las Vegas, it was named, in a play on the Hunter S. Thompson book: *Fear and Loving in Las Vegas*.

These are practical findings. Horror movies and romantic films are staples of the TV schedule. If you have an ad that uses either social proof or scarcity ensure it runs in the appropriate programming.

Just as there are advantages to tailoring your biases to the consumer that you're targeting, so are there advantages to tailoring the copy you use. In the next chapter I discuss the benefits, but also the pitfalls of personalisation.

BIAS 24

Cocktail Party Effect

The power of personalisation

> You end up listening to a couple of workmates gossiping about their recent night out. Halfway through the slightly rambling story, your ears prick up. Was that your name you heard from across the room?

IN THE EARLY 1950s, Colin Cherry had a similar experience. One evening, while chatting with friends at a party, he heard his name from across the room. Why, he wondered, was his name audible but not the rest of the conversation? It wasn't as if they had said his name any louder.

Cherry, a cognitive scientist at Imperial College, believed the quirk occurred because we're exposed to more information than we can consciously process. The subconscious deals with most of our sensory input; only a fraction is processed consciously. One of the ways our brains determine what is worthy of conscious attention is personal relevance – this is termed the *cocktail party effect*.

The media landscape is like a packed pub

Cherry's theory is of interest to advertisers as it solves one of their biggest problems: being noticed.

A few years ago, the *Guardian* quantified the proportion of ads we recall. They equipped a journalist with an eye-tracking headset, which monitored all the ads he was exposed to, and sent him off to walk around London. After a few hours, he was asked to list all the ads he recalled; they made up less than 1% of the total he was exposed to.

Cherry's work shows that personalisation is one way to grab attention. And it's easier than ever for advertisers to do that, now consumers leave a data trail online.

However, there are fundamental problems with the tactic.

Just because you can, doesn't mean you should

Banner ads using a customer's name are noticeable, but they're also unpalatable. Consumers are disturbed by advertisers assuming their personal data is public property. Of the 304 people I surveyed 36% complained that personalised banner ads were completely unacceptable.

This is due to a lack of habituation, rather than intractable privacy concerns. Personalisation is acceptable in media such as direct mail, which has a long history of writing directly to individual customers. Only 23% of those questioned thought a personalised letter was unacceptable.

The aversion to personalisation will fade with time.

A furore accompanies the introduction of all new media. Newspaper ads seem innocuous enough to us. However, a reader of the *Times* complained about the "brutal vulgarity" of running ads next to editorial when the paper began the practice in 1892. Previously the ads had been sectioned off at the back of the paper.

In 1952 Lord Reith, founder of the BBC, famously compared the prospect of commercial TV to smallpox and the Black Death. Even the harshest critic wouldn't agree ITV turned out that bad.

The aversion to personalisation will fade with time. However, that doesn't help current campaigns that need to deal with the world as it is, not as it might one day be.

The second problem is that personalisation, when you get it wrong, is jarring. Unfortunately, this is a common occurrence as data used for targeting is often flawed.

> # Localisation is relevant enough to attract attention, without being personal enough to offend.

When writing this chapter, I looked at the data Google use to target me. You can find out yours by going to www.google.com/settings/u/o/ads. Google assumes I'm a 35-44 year old male. Spot on. They've also correctly identified that I'm interested in trainers, coffee, folk music and football. However, they mistakenly believe I'm interested in combat sports, trucks and boating.

These mistakes are troubling. Charles Vallance, founder of ad agency VCCP, says:

> Being wide of the mark is much worse than being wrong. It's like calling a Yorkshire man a Lancastrian, just because the counties are adjacent. It's like the bloke in front of me in Starbucks who got "Pies" written on his cup when it should have been "Piers".

How to apply this effect

1. Adopt a softer approach

Considering the dangers of personalisation, brands should be relevant, without being intrusive. That's a tricky balance, but one that localisation achieves. Localisation is relevant enough to attract attention, without being personal enough to offend.

An experiment by JC Decaux demonstrated the strength of this approach. They ran two posters for a broadband provider. One version related the offer to the UK, the other to the site of the ad, Charing Cross station. The locally tailored activity generated 14% higher spontaneous awareness than the nationwide message.

2. Bridging the trust gap

Localisation has benefits beyond improved recall. I told 500 nationally representative consumers about a fictitious new energy tariff. Half the participants were informed that it saved the average household £100, the other half that it saved households in their city the same amount.

When the message was regionally tailored, 10% of participants agreed that the offer was great value, compared to only 4% for the national message. A minor copy tweak had doubled the impact.

This shows that localisation boosts impact as well as recall.

But why?

It may be that consumers are cynical about ad claims. According to an IPSOS Mori survey of 2,000 consumers, 38% claimed to seldom or never trust advertising. They ignore ads about generic, average savings as they suspect that vague claims may hide misleading statistics. A localised message assuages these worries as specific claims leave less room for deceit.

3. Charitable campaigns particularly benefit from localisation

Localisation may be of particular benefit to the charity sector, which suffers from the *bystander effect* – the idea that mass appeals for help suffer from a diffusion of responsibility.

The effect was first studied in the late 1960s by two psychologists, Bibb Latané and John Darley, from Columbia and Princeton University, respectively. They were inspired by one of the most infamous murders in New York's history, the brutal stabbing in 1964 of Kitty Genovese, which I mentioned earlier in the book. This violent incident was supposedly witnessed by either 37 or 38 people (the *New York Times* included both figures), none of whom intervened. The press interpreted this as symptomatic of the city's moral decline.

However, the psychologists took a different approach; the lack of intervention occurred because of, not despite, the volume of bystanders. To test their hypothesis, the psychologists faked a number of emergencies and monitored whether people were more likely to help if they were alone or in groups. In one such experiment, they recruited students for a survey about personal problems. While the student was completing the test, one of the researchers pretended to have an epileptic fit in a neighbouring room. Of the students who were alone, 85% went to help; this figure dropped to 31% when they were in groups of four.

Latané and Darley repeated the experiment with different types of emergencies. Each generated the same result: people in groups were less likely to help.

Charity appeals must create a sense that people are being asked individually. If asked en masse people think: why should I suffer the inconvenience and danger of helping, when others have also been asked?

If it's not possible to talk to people individually, localisation can partially counter the problem. An example of this was a project I worked on with the Give Blood campaign. Here the creative was adapted to highlight dwindling stocks in specific cities, rather than the country as a whole. This led to a marked improvement in response rates, as discussed earlier in the book.

4. Beware of brand scurvy

But can you have too much of a good thing? I met with Charles Vallance at his offices near London's Victoria Station to understand his concerns about personalisation. His worry is that while personalisation has a value in small doses, if you get the equilibrium between mass and personal communications wrong then it can be troublesome.

Vallance says:

> You have to create the brand aura for any personalisation to work. Otherwise it's just brand scurvy, it's feeding the brand all the wrong ingredients and all the wrong vitamins, and in the end it needs sunlight. Brands need mass exposure so that there's a common understanding about what it is and what the desirability hinges on.

As with so much in advertising, the trick is in getting the right balance.

5. Personal not personalised

It is possible to make the viewer feel they are being personally addressed without resorting to personalisation.

Perhaps the most famous example of a mass medium appealing directly to an individual is the World War One recruitment ad, featuring Lord Kitchener. According to Dave Trott:

> The army, fighting the Germans, was running out of soldiers so they ran a recruitment poster. But the visual didn't show massed ranks of soldiers with the headline, THE BRITISH ARMY IS SHORT OF TWO MILLION NEW RECRUITS.

> The visual was Kitchener pointing out of the poster, straight at the person looking at the poster. And the headline said YOUR COUNTRY NEEDS YOU. One-to-one. And that poster worked. It got millions of recruits, by talking to people one at a time.

This campaign, built around personal appeal, was so successful that the US government copied it during World War Two, where once again it recruited millions.

Bob Levenson, the copywriter behind many of the great Volkswagen ads, gave practical tips on how to adopt a personal tone of voice. He recommended imagining that you were writing your ads to a close friend:

> Start off with "Dear Charlie," then say "this is what I want to tell you about…". Make believe that the person you're talking to is a perfectly intelligent friend who knows less about the product than you do. Then, when you've finished writing the copy, just cross out "Dear Charlie".

Wise advice indeed.

For more advice, although maybe not quite so wise, turn to the next chapter where I'll be discussing the role of scarcity in making brands more appealing.

BIAS 25

Scarcity

The less there is, the more you want it

> You scan the menu and narrow your choice to steak. Now your dilemma is between the rib eye and the rump. The rump is cheaper, and you have an expensive night ahead, but the rib eye is tastier. You're still in a quandary when the waiter arrives.
>
> After running through the specials the waiter announces that unfortunately due to high demand, there are only two rib eyes left. You wonder if the rib eyes are particularly tasty if they're so popular. However, before you can open your mouth to order one, two of your colleagues beat you to it.

THE ALLURE OF items in short supply is not limited to steaks. The tendency of goods to become more appealing when there are limited numbers is known as the *scarcity bias*.

The most famous experiment into scarcity was led by Stephen Worchel, a psychologist at the University of Virginia. In 1975, he recruited 134 undergraduates and asked them to rate the quality of a batch of cookies. The participants tasted the cookies from a glass jar containing either ten or two biscuits. When the cookies were in scarce supply they were rated as significantly more likeable and attractive. The participants were also prepared to pay 11% more for them.

How to apply this effect

1. Limit the number of products that consumers can buy

It seems counter-intuitive but restricting the number of items customers can buy boosts sales. Brian Wansink, Professor of Marketing at Cornell University, investigated the effectiveness of this tactic in 1998. He persuaded three supermarkets in Sioux City, Iowa, to offer Campbell's soup at a small discount: 79c rather than 89c. The discounted soup was sold in one of three conditions: a control, where there was no limit on the volume of purchases, or two tests, where customers were limited to either four or twelve cans.

Restricting the number of items customers can buy boosts sales.

In the unlimited condition shoppers bought 3.3 cans on average, whereas in the scarce condition, when there was a cap, they bought 5.3 on average. This suggests scarcity encourages sales. The findings are particularly robust because the test took place in a supermarket with genuine shoppers. It didn't rely on claimed data, nor was it held in a laboratory where consumers might behave differently.

These scarce promotions are effective as they harness consumers' genuine feelings about brands. Shoppers believe retailers act self-interestedly, so if the supermarket limits sales there is an insinuation that the bargain is so good that it is losing that store money.

However, scarcity is not the only bias evident in Wansink's experiment. This is revealed if we split out the sales uplift in the two scarcity conditions. When consumers were limited to four cans they bought

3.5 on average but when the limit was a dozen, they purchased seven cans. A doubling of sales is a sizeable difference.

What is the explanation?

The answer lies in the concept of anchoring.

2. Ensure that the anchors that you communicate increases sales

Anchoring occurs when exposure to a number serves as a reference point for subsequent decisions. This occurs whether that number is relevant or not. The original evidence for anchoring came from Amos Tversky and Daniel Kahneman, psychologists who at the time were based at Hebrew University in Jerusalem. In 1974, they published their findings on a seemingly bizarre experiment in the journal *Science*.

The psychologists had recruited participants to spin a wheel of fortune. The wheel was rigged so that it stopped either on the number 10 or 65. Once the wheel came to a halt the spinners had to estimate what proportion of members of the United Nations were African countries. Those exposed to the higher number 65, estimated 45%, nearly double the guess for those seeing the lower number, which was on average 25%.

Even though the number on the wheel had no logical relevance to the answer, it influenced the participants by setting a starting point for their calculations. Those that had seen the lower number recognised that 10% was too low. 15% then? Probably still too low. 20%? Maybe. 25%? That sounds about right.

The same process was followed by those starting from a higher number. Again, they adjusted downwards and stopped at the first reasonable number they reached. Since the band of reasonable guesses for such a question is quite broad they stopped at a much higher number: 45%.

Anchoring affects commercial situations too. Gregory Northcraft and Margaret Neale from the University of Arizona ran an ingenious experiment in which estate agents were asked to value a home in

Tucson, Arizona. The estate agents were given a tour of the home and a pack of information on the house. They all received the same information apart from one element. Half were told the list price was $65,900 and half that it was $83,900.

Those who saw the low list price estimated the house's value at $67,811. In contrast, those who saw the higher anchor appraised the property at $75,190 on average. That's a swing of 11%, or more than $7,000. A considerable difference considering they were trained professionals. It suggests value is a slippery concept, only partially based on objective reality. If you work in professional services, it's delusional to think your clients weigh up your value dispassionately. Part of your perceived worth comes from the anchor, the initial price, you set.

What brands have harnessed this bias?

One campaign with anchoring at its heart is the far from romantic story of De Beers and their diamonds. During the first half of the 20th century there was no Western tradition for buying expensive diamond engagement rings. On the eve of World War Two only about 10% of engagement rings had diamonds, according to Citigroup. De Beers, who had a stranglehold on diamond supply, sought to change that with the help of the creative agency, N. W. Ayer.

They made two smart decisions. First, they positioned diamonds, the most durable stone, as a symbol of everlasting love. This was immortalised in the line, "A diamond is forever." Second, they encouraged heavy spending by setting a high anchor. They suggested a month's salary was the appropriate amount for an engagement ring. In the United States in the 1980s they doubled the norm with straplines such as, "Isn't two month's salary a small price to pay for something that lasts forever?" In Japan, they went further and suggested consumers pay three month's salary.

There is a reasonable case to be made that this is one of the most successful ads ever. Sales of diamonds in the United States alone rose from $23m to $2.1bn between 1939 and 1979.

3. Stress there is a limited time to buy your product

A simple way to apply the bias is to announce that if consumers don't purchase soon they'll miss out on the opportunity to do so.

This is an established tactic for brands, especially among retailers who often stress that a sale will end soon. However, brands are becoming increasingly sophisticated in their application of the bias. Ocado have introduced flash sales just before you checkout. The sale only lasts as long as you're on the page. The fleeting window available creates an abnormal level of interest in a half price tin of beans. As the author, G. K. Chesterton said, "The way to love anything is to realise that it might be lost."

> People feel losses more powerfully than the same level of gains.

It's not just retailers who benefit. Laura Maclean and I showed 300 consumers a poster for an upcoming film and asked them how likely they were to go and watch it that weekend. Half of the participants just saw the poster, while half were also told that it was finishing that weekend. Those who knew that time was limited were 36% more likely to act.

This is an opportunity as cinema-goers have little idea of how long films run. Simply promoting the end date would boost the attendees in the last few weeks.

One explanation for the appeal of scarce items is loss aversion – that people feel losses more powerfully than the same level of gains. Stressing the end date taps into this by emphasising that consumers are in danger of missing the opportunity.

Brands can apply this bias by tweaking their copy: rather than promoting their benefits, focus on what is being missed out by not switching. Working with Gabrielle Hobday, I surveyed 834 respondents to see how loss aversion could influence advertising claims. Half were told they could save £100 by switching to a new energy provider, while the remainder were informed they stood to lose £100 if they didn't switch.

The number who said they were very likely to switch rose from 7.4% in the first scenario to 10.7% in the second. A rise of 45%. Once again, emphasising the potential for loss makes a proposition more motivating.

These findings are interesting as most advertising claims about price communicate the savings. However, marketers can boost their effectiveness by re-framing their offers. Rather than stressing savings they should emphasise the loss involved by not taking up the offer.

This type of re-framing can be tested easily, and at limited cost, in search copy. If it works, then it can be extended to other communications.

4. Publicise that the short supply is due to high demand

Worchel's experiment had a final twist. Some participants were told that there were only two cookies in their jar as they had proved unexpectedly popular. In this scenario the cookies were rated highest of all. Participants were willing to pay 66p for the cookies compared to 46p in the control condition – an increase of 43%.

This element of the experiment suggests that explicitly mentioning the reason for scarcity is the ideal tactic for a brand. By doing so it applies two biases simultaneously: social proof and scarcity.

But if scarcity, and all the other biases we have discussed, are so powerful is it unethical to use them on unsuspecting consumers? It's a fair question. Let's address it in the next chapter.

Ethics

Why capitalising on biases is
both ethical and effective

> You stumble outside. You had promised yourself that
> you'd get a train home but it's far too late for that now.
>
> You scan the road for a taxi. The drizzle means taxis
> are hard to come by. After a tedious five-minute wait
> you flag one down. Within minutes you're fast asleep.
>
> You wake with a jolt as the taxi jerks to a halt outside
> your house.
>
> You scrabble through your pockets for some cash. A
> crumpled fiver and some shrapnel are not enough, so
> you'll have to pay by credit card. After fumbling with
> the card machine it prompts you to make a tip: 20%,
> 25% or 30% are the suggested amounts or you have
> the option to add your own figure.
>
> Unsure, you plump for 25%.

YOU'RE NOT ALONE in picking the middle option. Many
experiments have shown that this is the most popular choice. It
appeals as people fear being profligate or mean, and therefore, they
avoid the extremes.

But rather than discuss the magnetism of the middle, I want to use
this as an example of the ethics of nudging.

This topic has been of increasing interest. Lazar Dzamic, former Head of Brand Planning at Google ZOO, wrote an extended piece that summed up many of the arguments against nudging. Dzamic is by no means the only critic, but since his views have had some traction in the industry and because they cover the same points as other critics, I will focus on them.

His critique broadly fell into two camps. First, that nudging was too powerful:

> If behavioural economics is as powerful as we claim – the thing that warrants all those departments, institutes and even whole agencies popping up all the time – then it should be regulated for commercial purposes. No gung-ho, free-market BE for selling financial services, cars or fast food, unless the purveyors can prove they are beneficial, not detrimental, to consumers and the society at large.

And second, that it lacks transparency:

> The biases, collectively, contribute to the pervasive, default, irrational side of our nature so eloquently brought to light by Kahneman et al. It is exactly the side that we, the Mythocrats, try to exploit. If the cognitive biases are a sort of cognitive blindness, who wants to steal from the blind?

Let's deal with those complaints individually.

Dzamic's first criticism is that nudges are too powerful to be left in the hands of advertisers.

But is *powerful* the correct term? It suggests that nudges hypnotise a foolish public and beguile them into a particular course of action.

While many ad men crave that omnipotence, it's an exaggeration. The biases discussed throughout this book never sway everyone, all the time. They just increase the probability that communications have the desired effect. Nudges aren't occult magic; they merely improve ad effectiveness through an understanding of how the mind works.

If we accept that nudges don't bamboozle consumers, then what really is the complaint? That the communications are successful? Surely, if ads for a product are permitted, you can't then object to them being effective?

David Halpern, CEO of the Nudge Unit, says:

> If we think it's appropriate and acceptable for such communications to occur, it seems sensible to expect those designing or writing them to make them effective and easy to understand.

And if it's powerful communications that Dzamic objects to, why single out behavioural economics? Why not object to the great creative that has nothing to do with behavioural science: the Cadbury Gorilla, the meerkat, or the 118 118 runners.

But to be fair to him, it's not just the power he worries about; rather it's the unregulated power. But this is a misnomer: behavioural ads are regulated. They're regulated like every other piece of commercial communication. The Advertising Standards Authority insists all ads are: "legal, decent, honest and truthful". They do not make exceptions for behavioural ads.

But what about the lack of transparency?

If Dzamic's first objection about behavioural science is unsubstantiated, then what of his second concern, the lack of transparency? If people are unaware that these biases are occurring, then is this malevolent manipulation?

Once again let's unpick the exact argument. What does a lack of transparency mean? I think there are only two plausible complaints. First, consumers are being fooled by only seeing a biased selection of information, rather than all of it. Second, consumers are being swayed by more than pure logic; that nudging appeals to our irrational side.

The first point, that many nudges show a limited selection of options, is true. Take the taxi example, where only three options, from an infinite possibility, are spelt out: a tip of 20%, 25% or 30%. However, the inference that this selectivity is immoral is flawed.

Every piece of communication is selective. Imagine if that taxi had given you every option. A 1% tip, a 2% tip, a 3% tip and so on and so on. In fact, why stop there. For the message to be truly comprehensive it would have had to give far more options: a 1.0% tip, a 1.1% tip and so on, ad nauseam. The complexity would have been bewildering.

The ludicrousness of requiring all information to be shown is dramatised by the short story, *On Exactitude in Science* by Jorge Louis Borges, the Argentine writer. His story tells of an Empire unhappy with the impreciseness of their maps. Until one day when, as Borges says, the:

> Cartographers Guilds struck a Map of the Empire whose size was that of the Empire, and which coincided point for point with it.

Of course, when they build this map it's pointless; an unwieldy duplication of reality. Years later, the map has rotted in the sun:

> In the Deserts of the West, still today, there are Tattered Ruins of that Map, inhabited by Animals and Beggars; in all the Land there is no other Relic of the Disciplines of Geography.

In the same way, communications that leave nothing out are futile. Any ad or piece of communication must be selective. And once you start selecting information it can't be neutral. Any set of facts will be from a particular perspective. There is no getting away from that. As Rory Sutherland says:

> The process is inevitable. Criticising nudging is like criticising electromagnetism or gravity – the best we can do is be aware of the forces at work, to understand them and to make people widely aware of them.

The second element of the transparency critique is that persuasive techniques other than cold logic are being deployed. That's true, but so what?

More than two thousand years ago Aristotle wrote down advice for those seeking to persuade. *The Art of Rhetoric* outlines three broad requirements for effective persuasion: logos, ethos and pathos.

Logos, or the application of reason and logic, is important but ineffective alone. It needs to be complemented by ethos, an appeal based on the character of the speaker, and pathos, an appeal to emotions. Facts fall flat if delivered dryly.

> ## Facts fall flat if delivered dryly.

That an audience is moved by emotional pleas doesn't make them blind; it makes them human.

If nudging, like rhetoric, is merely a tool then what matters is to what ends you harness it. Are you selling snake-oil? Or are you selling something of substance? If it's the former, then no defence of the techniques you're using justifies it.

How to apply this effect

Nudge for the long term

Nudges can be used in such a wide range of circumstances that it's difficult to provide universal rules. The closest I have found is to nudge for the long term.

Most marketers want customers to be prepared to pay a premium for their brand again and again. The best way to achieve that is to ensure that no nudge leaves people feeling they haven't got fair value from the transaction.

But what does that mean in practice?

Well, think back to the taxi example. Our social norm is that a tip of about 10% is fair. So, steering people to pay double, or triple, that amount generates short-term income, but also long-term problems.

It leaves customers bitter. And those irritated customers will bad-mouth your brand and stop buying. You've sacrificed the long-term health of your brand for a quick quid.

If a nudge doesn't help the long-term health of your brand it is worth reconsidering using it.

A real-world example that irritates me is from the shower gel I used to use. They increased the diameter of the aperture on the bottle, probably on the assumption that people don't carefully weigh up the amount of gel they use. Instead consumers get in the habit of giving the bottle a quick squeeze for a set amount of time. By increasing the diameter, the washer ends up with far more gel than they need. To begin with it probably looks like a great tactic: sales increase as consumers get through their supplies more quickly. But the long-term impact will be less positive as shoppers become aware they have been conned and move onto other brands.

Anyone who works in marketing should recognise that sometimes the best long-term route is to sacrifice short-term gains. If a nudge doesn't help the long-term health of your brand it is worth reconsidering using it.

Conclusion

D o you remember the story of Kitty Genovese I mentioned in the Introduction and Bias 24? She was the 28-year-old who was murdered while none of the 37 (or 38) witnesses intervened. It was a brutal incident – but some good came from it. It inspired Latané and Darley to begin their research into the bystander effect and it even kick-started the establishment of a single number, 911, for calling the police.

But you may be surprised to learn that these important consequences were in fact based on a lie. Yes, Winston Moseley murdered Genovese in 1964, but the apathy that so enraged the *New York Times* was grossly exaggerated.

Nearly fifty years after the stabbing, the *New York Post* published evidence from Kevin Cook that discredited the original press reports. Not all the witnesses were as apathetic as suggested. One neighbour, Robert Mozer, witnessed Moseley's initial attack and leaned out of his seventh-floor window, yelling, "Leave that girl alone". His intervention sent the attacker scurrying away and gave Genovese the chance to stagger off. Mozer assumed the problem was over and returned to bed. Unfortunately, Moseley was not so easily deterred, and he tracked the injured Genovese down to launch another – this time fatal – attack.

Another witness, Samuel Hoffman, called the police and told them a woman "got beat up and was staggering around". No patrol car came. And finally, another neighbour, Sophie Farrar, was concerned enough to run to the vestibule – the site of the final attack. Considering Farrar didn't know whether Moseley had fled, it was a remarkably brave intervention, especially for someone who was four feet eleven tall.

Unfortunately, by the time she arrived, Genovese was close to death and all she could do was comfort Genovese as her life ebbed away.

The actions of these three witnesses shows that the truth was far more complex than the *New York Times* insinuated.

The developments in the Kitty Genovese case are an appropriate end to this book, as they provide lessons on how to use the biases I have outlined.

The story suggests that we should maintain a healthy scepticism about the explanations we hear. We should be wary of anecdotes when explaining behaviour. We often mistake the interest and excitement of a story for the truth.

Gripping though the *New York Times* article may have been, it was misleading. The more nuanced truth about human behaviour was revealed by the rigorous scientific experimentation of Latané and Darley. We would do well to remember this in advertising and give more weight to credible, evidence-based explanations of behaviour – based on psychology or behavioural science, for example – than catchy anecdotes.

Finally, the story alerts us to the danger of an uncritical acceptance of claims by others. However compelling a tale is, it isn't necessarily true. This leads us to one of behavioural science's greatest strengths. The principles I have highlighted in this book do not need to be taken on faith alone; you can create experiments to ensure they work for your brand. The modern digital world has made it cheaper and easier than ever to conduct simple tests.

I think behavioural science is the best way to understand human behaviour.

But don't take my word for it. Go and test it for yourself.

References

Introduction

'37 Who Saw Murder Didn't Call the Police', *New York Times*, 27 March 1964

'Effect of colour of drugs: systematic review of perceived effect of drugs and of their effectiveness', by Anton J M de Craen, Pieter J Roos, A Leonard de Vries, Jos Kleijnen [*British Medical Journal*, Vol. 313; 21 Dec 1996]

How Brands Grow by Byron Sharp [2010]

The Wiki Man by Rory Sutherland [2011]

Bias 1: The fundamental attribution error

'From Jerusalem to Jericho', by John Darley and Daniel Batson [*Journal of Personality and Social Psychology*, Vol. 27, No. 1, pp. 100–108, 1973]

Marketers Are from Mars, Consumers Are from New Jersey by Bob Hoffman [2015]

'Social Roles, Social Control, and Biases in Social-Perception Processes', by Lee Ross, Teresa Amabile, and Julia Steinmetz [*Journal of Personality and Social Psychology*, Vol. 35, No. 7, pp. 485–494, 1977]

Bias 2: Social proof

Influence: Science and Practice by Robert Cialdini [1984]

Behind the Scenes in Advertising: More Bull More (Mark III) [2003]

Bias 3: Negative social proof

'Crafting Normative Messages to Protect the Environment', by Robert Cialdini [*Current Directions in Psychological Science*, Vol. 12, No. 4, pp. 105–109, 2003]

Inside the Nudge Unit: How Small Changes Can Make a Big Difference by David Halpern [2015]

'Perils of Perception: A Fourteen Country Study' by IPSOS MORI [2014]

Bias 4: Distinctiveness

'Aging and the von Restorff Isolation Effect in Short/Term Memory', by Richard Cimbalo and Lois Brink [*The Journal of General Psychology*, Vol. 106, No. 1, pp. 69–76, 1982]

Bias 5: Habit

'Habits in Everyday Life: Thought, Emotion, and Action', by Wendy Wood, Jeffrey Quinn and Deborah Kashy [*Journal of Personality and Social Psychology*, Vol. 83, No. 6, pp. 1281–1297, 2002]

'Sainsbury's – How an idea helped make Sainsbury's great again', by Tom Roach, Craig Mawdsley and Jane Dorsett [IPA Effectiveness Awards 2008]

'People Search for Meaning When They Approach a New Decade in Chronological Age', by Adam Alter and Hal Hershfield [*Proceedings of the National Academy of Sciences of the United States of America*, Vol. 111, No. 48, pp. 17066–17070, 2014]

Inside the Nudge Unit: How Small Changes Can Make a Big Difference by David Halpern [2015]

Bias 6: The pain of payment

'Always Leave Home Without It: A Further Investigation of the Credit-Card Effect on Willingness to Pay', by Drazen Prelec and Duncan Simester [*Marketing Letters*, Vol. 12, No. 1, pp. 5–12, 2001]

'$ or Dollars: Effects of Menu-Price Formats on Restaurant Checks', by Sybil Yang, Sheryl Kimes and Mauro Sessarego [*Cornell Hospitality Report*, Vol. 9, No. 8, pp. 6–11, 2009]

'"The Best Price You'll Ever Get": The 2005 Employee Discount Pricing Promotions in the U.S. Automobile Industry', by Meghan Busse, Duncan Simester and Florian Zettelmeyer [*Marketing Science*, Vol. 29, No. 2, pp. 268–290, 2008]

Bias 7: The danger of claimed data

Dataclysm: Who We Are When We Think No-one's Looking by Christian Rudder [2014]

'The Influence of In-store Music on Wine Selections', by Adrian North, David Hargreaves and Jennifer Kendrick [*Journal of Applied Psychology*, Vol. 84, No. 2, pp. 271–276, 1999]

The Righteous Mind: Why Good People are Divided by Politics and Religion by Jonathan Haidt [2012]

'The National Survey of Sexual Attitudes and Lifestyles', UCL, London School of Tropical Medicine and Hygiene, and National Research Centre [2010–2012]

Everybody Lies: Big Data, New Data, and What the Internet Can Tell Us About Who We Really Are by Seth Stephens-Davidowitz [2017]

Bias 8: Mood

'In the Mood for Advertising', by Fred Bronner, Jasper Bronner and John Faasse [*International Journal of Advertising*, Vol. 26, No. 3, 2007]

'Inferring Negative Emotion from Mouse Cursor Movements', by Martin Hibbeln, Jeffrey Jenkins, Christoph Schneider, Joseph S. Valacich, and Markus Weinmann [*MIS Quarterly*, Vol. 41, No.1, pp. 1–21, 2017]

'Consumers' Response to Commercials: When the Energy Level in the Commercial Conflicts with the Media Context', by Nancy

Puccinelli, Keith Wilcox, and Dhruv Grewal [*Journal of Marketing*, Vol. 79, No. 2, pp. 1–18, 2015]

Bias 9: Price relativity

The Wiki Man by Rory Sutherland [2011]

'Context-Dependent Preferences', by Amos Tversky and Itamar Simonson [*Management Science*, Vol. 39, No. 10, pp. 1179–1189, 1993]

Bias 10: Primacy effect

'Forming Impressions of Personality', by Solomon Asch [*Journal of Abnormal Psychology*, Vol. 41, pp. 258–290, 1946]

Bias 11: Expectancy theory

Mindless Eating by Brian Wansink [2006]

Bias 12: Confirmation bias

'On resistance to persuasive communications', by Leon Festinger and Nathan Maccoby [*The Journal of Abnormal and Social Psychology*, Vol. 68, No. 4, pp. 359–366, 1964]

Seducing the Subconscious: The Psychology of Emotional Influence in Advertising by Robert Heath [2012]

'They Saw a Game: A Case Study', by Albert Hastorf and Hadley Cantril [*Journal of Abnormal Psychology*, Vol. 49, No. 1, pp. 129–134, 1954]

Bias 13: Overconfidence

'Unskilled and Unaware of It: How Difficulties in Recognizing One's Own Incompetence Lead to Inflated Self-Assessments', by Justin Kruger and David Dunning [*Journal of Personality and Social Psychology*, Vol. 77, No. 6, pp. 1121–1134, 1999]

'Are We All Less Risky and More Skillful Than Our Fellow Drivers?', by Ola Svenson [*Acta Psychologica*, Vol. 47, pp. 143–148, 1981]

The Wiki Man by Rory Sutherland [2011]

Psychology of Intelligence Analysis by Richards Heuer [1999]

Bias 14: Wishful seeing

'Value and Need as Organizing Factors in Perception', by Jerome Bruner and Cecile Goodman [*Journal of Abnormal and Social Psychology*, Vol. 42, pp. 33–44, 1947]

Grow: How Ideals Power Growth and Profit at the World's Greatest Companies by Jim Stengel and Marc Cashman [2011]

The Halo Effect by Phil Rosenzweig [2007]

Bias 15: Media context

weirderthanyouthink.wordpress.com/tag/daniel-dennett

'Evidence for a neural correlate of a framing effect: bias-specific activity in the ventromedial prefrontal cortex during credibility judgments', by M. Deppe, W. Schwindt, J. Krämer, H. Kugel, H. Plassmann, P. Kenning, E. Ringelstein, [*Brain Research Bulletin*, Vol. 67, No. 5, pp. 413–421, 2005]

Behind the Scenes in Advertising: More Bull More (Mark III) [2003]

'Is advertising rational?', by Evan Davis, John Kay, and Jonathan Star [*London Business School Review*, Vol. 2, No. 3, pp. 1–23, 1991]

Marketers Are from Mars, Consumers Are from New Jersey by Bob Hoffman [2015]

Bias 16: The curse of knowledge

Made to Stick: Why Some Ideas Survive and Others Die by Chip Heath and Dan Heath [2008]

The Wiki Man by Rory Sutherland [2011]

Bias 17: Goodhart's law

Long and Short of It: Balancing Short- and Long-Term Marketing Strategies by Les Binet and Peter Field [2012]

Management in 10 Words by Terry Leahy [2012]

Leading by Alex Ferguson and Michael Moritz [2015]

Bias 18: The pratfall effect:

Social Animal by Elliot Aronson [1972]

The Wasp Factory by Iain Banks [1984]

Bias 19: Winner's curse

The Winner's Curse: Paradoxes and Anomalies of Economic Life by Richard Thaler [1991]

Originals: How Non-Conformists Move the World by Adam Grant [2016]

'Harnessing naturally occurring data to measure the response of spending to income', by Michael Gelman, Shachar Kariv, Matthew Shapiro, Dan Silverman, Steven Tadelis [*Science*, Vol. 345, No. 6193, pp. 212–215, 2014]

'The Psychology of Windfall Gains', by Hal Arkes, Cynthia Joyner, Mark Pezzo, Jane Gradwohl Nash, Karen Siegel-Jacobs, Eric Stone Eric [*Organizational Behaviour and Human Decision Processes*, Vol. 59, No. 3, pp. 331–347, 1994]

On the Fungibility of Spending and Earnings – Evidence from Rural China and Tanzania by Luc Christiaensen and Lei Pan [2012]

Bias 20: The power of the group

'Humour in Television Advertising: The Effects of Repetition and Social Setting', by Yong Zhang and George Zinkhan [*Advances In Consumer Research*, Vol. 18, pp. 813–818, 1991]

'Feeling More Together: Group Attention Intensifies Emotion', by Garriy Shteynberg, Jacob Hirsh, Evan Apfelbaum, Jeff Larsen, Adam Galinsky, and Neal Roese [*Emotion*, Vol. 14, No. 6, pp. 1102–1114, 2014]

Bias 21: Veblen goods

'Commercial Features of Placebo and Therapeutic Efficacy', by Rebecca Waber, Baba Shiv, Ziv Carmon; Dan Ariely [*Journal of the American Medical Association*, Vol. 299, No.9, pp. 1016–1017, 2008]

Bias 22: The replicability crisis

'Why Susie Sells Seashells by the Seashore: Implicit Egotism and Major Life Decisions', by Brett Pelham, Matthew Mirenberg, and John Jones [*Journal of Personality and Social Psychology*, Vol. 82, No. 4, pp. 469–487, 2002]

'Rich the banker? What's not in a Name', by Tim Harford [2016], www.timharford.com/2016/11/rich-the-banker-whats-not-in-a-name

'Estimating the reproducibility of psychological science', by Brian Nosek et al. [*Science*, Vol. 349, No. 6251, 2015]

'Comment on "Estimating the reproducibility of psychological science"', by Daniel Gilbert, Gary King, Stephen Pettigrew and Timothy Wilson [*Science*, Vol. 351, Issue 6277, p. 1037, 2016]

'Meta-assessment of bias in science', by Daniele Fanelli, Rodrigo Costats, and John Ioannidis [*Proceedings of the National Academy of Sciences*, Vol. 114, No. 14, pp. 3714–3719, 2017]

'Evaluating replicability of laboratory experiments in economics', by Colin F. Camerer et al. [*Science*, Vol. 351, No. 6280, pp. 1433–1436, 2016]

Bias 23: Variability

Inside the Nudge Unit: How Small Changes Can Make a Big Difference by David Halpern [2015]

'Fear and Loving in Las Vegas: Evolution, Emotion, and Persuasion', by Vladas Griskevicius, Noah Goldstein, Chad R. Mortensen, Jill Sundie, Robert Cialdini and Douglas Kenrick [*Journal of Market Research*, Vol. 46, No. 3, pp. 384–395, 2009]

Bias 24: Cocktail party effect

The shocking history of advertising! by E. S. Turner [1953]

'Bystander Intervention in Emergencies: Diffusion of Responsibility', by John Darley and Bibb Latané [*Journal of Personality and Social Psychology*, Vol. 8, No. 4, pp. 377–383, 1968]

Creative Mischief by Dave Trott [2009]

Ugly Is Only Skin-Deep: The Story of the Ads That Changed the World by Dominik Imseng [2016]

Bias 25: Scarcity

'Effects of Supply and Demand on Ratings of Object Value', by Stephen Worchel, Jerry Lee and Akanbi Adewole [*Journal of Personality and Social Psychology*, Vol. 32, No. 5, pp. 906–914, 1975]

Mindless Eating by Brian Wansink [2006]

Thinking, Fast and Slow by Daniel Kahneman [2011]

Why Smart People Make Big Money Mistakes and How to Correct Them: Lessons From The New Science of Behavioural Economics by Gary Belsky and Thomas Gilovich [1999]

Ethics

'Should Behavioural Economics in marketing be regulated – or hyped-down?', by Lazar Dzamic, www.bobcm.net/2017/01/21/should-behavioural-economics-in-marketing-be-regulated-or-hyped-down

Inside the Nudge Unit: How Small Changes Can Make a Big Difference by David Halpern [2015],

'The Dishonesty of Honest People: A Theory of Self-Concept Maintenance', by Nina Mazar, On Amir, Dan Ariely [*Journal of Marketing Research*, Vol. 45, No. 6, pp.633–644, 2008]. SSRN ID: 979648

Conclusion

'Debunking the myth of Kitty Genovese', *New York Post*, 16 February 2014

Further reading

The Social Animal [Elliot Aronson, 1972]

First, make sure you buy the right book – confusingly there are two psychology books called *The Social Animal*, one by David Brooks the other by Elliot Aronson. Aronson's book is out of print and currently second-hand copies cost £40 on Amazon. However, if you're patient you should be able to get your hands on one for £20.

Aronson's own research covered cognitive dissonance and the pratfall effect but this book covers a far broader range of biases.

Decoded: The Science Behind Why We Buy [Phil Barden, 2013]

Most books on behavioural science talk about the subject in general terms, relying on the reader to figure out how they'll apply it to marketing. *Decoded* was one of the first books to address that gap. It covers a broad range of experiments and suggests how they can be applied to marketing.

Influence [Robert Cialdini, 1984]

This is one of the classics of social psychology. Robert Cialdini, Professor of Psychology at Arizona State University, outlines six biases that shape human behaviour, namely: reciprocity, commitment, social proof, authority, liking and scarcity.

The Art of Thinking Clearly [Rolf Dobelli, 2013]

Dobelli's book has 99 chapters, each dedicated to a specific bias. Since his chapters are only three to four pages long it makes for a remarkably easy read. It's not as authoritative as the other books listed here, but what it lacks in depth it makes up for in breadth. Dobelli's other strength is an eye for a good anecdote.

Copy, Copy, Copy: How to Do Smarter Marketing by Using Other People's Ideas [Mark Earls, 2015]

Most of the books I have recommended cover a broad range of biases. This book is different as it focusses on just one bias: social proof. It shows that people don't make decisions in isolation but are strongly influenced by their peers.

The strength of the book is that it's full of practical recommendations and lots of interesting examples of how brands have harnessed the social nature of their customers.

Inside the Nudge Unit [David Halpern, 2015]

This is an excellent book written by the CEO of the Behavioural Insight Team, the organisation set up to apply behavioural science to government policy. It outlines four broad approaches to: make it easy, attractive, social and timely. These themes are just as applicable to commercial advertising as government advertising.

Many books on nudges and biases just recount the results of academic experiments. This stands out as it provides lots of details about real-world tests that government departments have run.

Consumer.ology: The Truth About Consumers and the Psychology of Shopping [Philip Graves, 2010]

David Ogilvy famously said, "People don't think how they feel. They don't say what they think and they don't do what they say." Graves proves this is true and outlines the implications for market research.

Thinking, Fast and Slow [Daniel Kahneman, 2011]

Kahneman won the Nobel Prize for Economics in 2002 for his work on behavioural economics with Amos Tversky. This book gives an overview of his major ideas.

It's not as easy to read as the other titles I've listed. Jordan Ellenberg, a professor at the University of Wisconsin-Madison, analysed data from Amazon's Kindle to estimate how much of a book was read by the average reader. By looking at how the top highlighted passages were spread through the book he calculated when people had stopped reading. By his estimate readers only got 6.8% through Thinking, Fast and Slow. That's a shame as it's well worth persevering.

Priceless: The Hidden Psychology of Value [William Poundstone, 2010]

Priceless focuses on the psychology of value. The benefit of this angle is that it covers fresh areas that other books ignore. My favourite part was his discussion of how restaurants design menus to decrease price sensitivity.

If you enjoy the topic of pricing, I'd also recommend Leigh Caldwell's *The Psychology of Price: How to Use Price to Increase Demand, Profit and Customer Satisfaction*.

The Person and the Situation [Lee Ross and Richard Nisbett, 1991]

Malcolm Gladwell admitted that: "All of my books have been, in some sense, intellectual godchildren of *The Person and the Situation*". What more do you need from a recommendation?

Behavioural Insights Team Reports

This is a fascinating collection of government experiments conducted by the Behavioural Insight Team. Their annual reports are full of examples of behavioural principles being applied and the results.

One of the unique elements of the reports is that they discuss what didn't work as well as what did. Another strength is the analysis of what makes for a robust test.

The 2015–16 report can be downloaded for free here: www.behaviouralinsights.co.uk/publications/the-behavioural-insights-teams-update-report-2015-16

The Wiki Man [Rory Sutherland, 2011]

This is probably my favourite book on behavioural science and certainly the only one I have read three times. It's also the funniest.

Many of the advertising applications for behavioural science are pretty straightforward. The brilliance of this book is that Sutherland takes the same biases that everyone else knows about and applies them in wonderfully unique ways.

Sutherland also writes a fortnightly blog for *The Spectator*. It's ostensibly a technology column but it often covers behavioural science. If you prefer videos to the written word then watch his many TED talks, starting with 'Life Lessons from an Ad Man'.

Irrationality [Stuart Sutherland, 1992]

If I had to recommend just one pure psychology book, it'd be this. It was written by Sutherland, the Professor of Experimental Psychology at the University of Sussex, a full 16 years before *Nudge*.

Somehow, in the early 2000s, it went out of print. Before it was re-issued second hand copies were so sought after that they traded for a hundred quid. It's a wide-ranging book, covering a huge range of biases. Whatever brief you're working on there'll be a relevant experiment in here. Best of all it's a joy to read.

Mindless Eating: Why We Eat More Than We Think [Brian Wansink, 2006]

After a while psychology books can become a little repetitive. You need to wade through a lot of familiar experiments until you find a fresh one.

However, this book by Wansink, a psychologist at Cornell University, is strikingly different as it focuses on one specific area: the psychology of food. The other strength of the book is the creativity that Wansink shows in creating tests to prove his hypotheses.

Acknowledgements

One of the most enjoyable aspects of writing the book was interviewing a selection of experienced and knowledgeable people in the ad industry. These included Rory Sutherland, Vic Polkinghorne, Ian Leslie, Lucy Jameson, Mark Earls, Charles Vallance, Leigh Caldwell and Owain Service. Their insights were invaluable.

Dave Trott has been particularly generous with his time in providing memorable quotes, which have helped me understand the advertising application of the biases covered in the book.

The book covers many years' worth of experiments. These experiments would not have been possible without the hard work and skills of many people, in particular Jenny Riddell, Claire Linford, Rebecca Strong and Anna Kandasamy.

The structure and flow of the book have been significantly improved by the editing of Stephen Eckett at Harriman House. Without his advice to focus on the application of the biases the book would have been less distinctive.

Finally, thanks to my wife, Jane, and two children, Tom and Anna. Jane radically improved the style and substance of the initial drafts and both my children have reminded me to keep things simple. Good advice for a book, not bad for an ad either.

Index

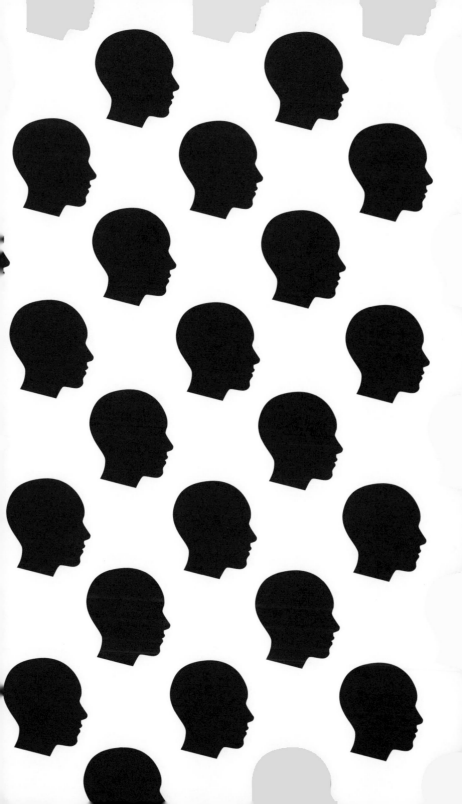